101

DESKTOP PUBLISHING AND GRAPHICS PROGRAMS

Patrick R. Dewey

AMERICAN LIBRARY ASSOCIATION
Chicago and London   1993

Series Note

This is the fourth work in the "101 MICRO Series" for librarians. The purpose of these books is to make very basic and useful information available about microcomputers in libraries. These books are designed specifically for the manager and staff of small to medium libraries.

Other books in this series

101 Software Packages to Use in Your Library
101 Microcomputer Projects to Do in Your Library
202 + Software Packages to Use in Your Library

Managing Editor Joan A. Grygel

Cover designed by Charles Bozett

Composed by Alexander Typesetting, Inc., in Times Roman and Helvetica on Datalogics

Printed on 50-pound Glatfelter, a pH-neutral stock, and bound in 10-point C1S cover stock by BookCrafters

The paper used in this publication meets the minimum requirements of American National Standard for Information Sciences—Permanence of Paper for Printed Library Materials, ANSI Z39.48-1984.∞

Library of Congress Cataloging-in-Publication Data

Dewey, Patrick R., 1949–
    101 desktop publishing and graphics programs / by Patrick R. Dewey.
        p. cm.—(101 micro series)
    Includes bibliographical references.
    ISBN 0-8389-0606-0
    1. Desktop publishing—Software—Catalogs. 2. Computer graphics—Software—Catalogs. 3. Computer art—Software—Catalogs. I. Title. II. Title: One hundred one desktop publishing and graphics programs. III. Title: One hundred and one desktop publishing and graphics programs. IV. Series.
Z253.53.D48   1993
686.2'2544536—dc20   93-13642

Printed in the United States of America.

97 96 95 94 93   5 4 3 2 1

This book is in loving memory of
Wilbur "Joe" Dewey

Contents

Introduction

Libraries, like most businesses, market or advertize their services to their public. They create newsletters, brochures, banners, and flyers for general distribution and publication of library events. They also generate many graphics products for children's programs such as puzzles, announcements, greeting cards, and booklets for reading programs. Some libraries create their own bookmarks, stationery letterheads, and business cards. A few ambitious librarians even create their own library handbooks and personnel manuals. Since many libraries have few funds for such activities, this means marketing innovatively and creatively—i.e., at low cost. Few libraries can afford the expense of typesetting. They have always used scissors and paper and glue for physically cutting and pasting documents—text and graphics—together. The final camera-ready copy was then duplicated in one way or another, sometimes by mimeograph, sometimes by a print shop down the street.

Then, microcomputers and software appeared, and the world changed forever. Computing brought with it four major improvements for library work. (1) Work that used to take days could now be completed in perhaps one short session. (2) The quality of the finished product could look much more professional than handmade materials. (3) Librarians could now choose from a much greater variety of production elements (e.g., artwork, typefaces, headlines, columns, etc.). (4) Materials in production could be viewed in a variety of formats prior to printing.

There is a staggering array of microcomputer brands, models, and add-on devices available. With minor exceptions, microcomputers fit into three categories: the IBM and its clones or compatibles that dominate the market, the Apple Macintosh computer, and the Apple II. The Apple II, the first microcomputer ever developed, is quickly fading from the scene, but it still exists in large numbers. Although it will perform many library functions quite well for some libraries, it is generally classed as a machine for school and educational uses.

The IBM class of microcomputers uses the DOS text-based disk operating system. A command is entered, and the machine will perform a task or run a program. These are far more powerful than the Apple IIs, but they still use the same style of operating system.

The Apple Macintosh was a response to the IBM. As it turns out, it was a totally radical approach to modern computing. The operating system became known as a graphic user interface (GUI), which is graphics based instead of text based. This style of system puts a user-friendly layer between the not-so-friendly DOS and the computer user. It is a complete break with the original DOS system. To explain a GUI it is necessary to explain a mouse, clicking, and icons. The mouse is a small hand-held device that is used to move the cursor around the screen with great ease to make menu selections and manipulate data. A mouse also can be used to draw lines and images in a drawing program more easily than most other possible forms of data entry. When the pointer has been moved to the proper menu item, a button on the mouse is clicked to select the menu item. Menu selections are not represented by names as columns of text spelling out the program names; instead, they are small graphic elements (pictures) called *icons* that represent programs and files. Users do not have to type a program name to run a program. They just click the mouse and the program is activated. With a GUI it is possible to have more than one program running at a time. The GUI opens a window for each program that has been selected and the user then jumps back and forth between them as necessary. The Macintosh's graphic orientation also signaled the birth of true desktop publishing; that is, the creation of whole pages with text and graphics mixed together.

The IBM class of computers has clearly changed direction since the development of the GUI and has caught up with the Macintosh. Microsoft's Windows gives the DOS-based machine a window environment that is just as capable as the Macintosh when it comes to desktop publishing or any other task. Windows is a well-developed working environment. In addition to using Windows, IBM users still have access to DOS if they so desire.

When looking for software for DOS computers, there may be several versions available. WordPerfect, for example, is sold in a DOS version and a Windows version. There are usually important differences in two such versions. Most notably, a Windows version will piggy-back on the back of Windows, taking advantage of the many features of the graphics operating system including the mouse, pull-down menus, and the icon filing system. It will also start up from the Windows menu. DOS versions often require that Windows be exited to operate the program.

Despite all of the hoopla about the type of microcomputer that is best, an equally important component of hardware is the selection of add-on devices. The most important of these is the printer. For the most-impressive graphics the only choice is the laser printer. PostScript is a page description language developed by Adobe Systems. It tells the computer how to print a complete page with text and graphics. It is device independent though widely used with laser printers. This high-quality printer is now within the price range of most users, at least on the low end. A low-end laser printer is like a low-end copy machine; they both have few additional features beyond the basic printing and copying. A high-end laser printer will print faster and have more memory, selection of papers, etc. On the high end, a laser printer can still easily cost many thousands of dollars.

Other components of a desktop system may include various types of scanners, devices that convert type, photos, and video images to computer use. A picture or other graphic item on paper can be fed into a scanner and converted into a computer file for use with many of the programs listed in this book. (A word of caution about scanning is in order. Since any picture can be scanned, this does not mean that it is okay to do so. Copyright still applies. People who scan should only scan their own materials or have permission from the copyright owner.) It becomes, in effect, clip art. The number and variety of printers, modems, monitors, and even internal enhancements, such as color graphics boards, that can be coupled to a microcomputer system is almost endless.

Hundreds of computer programs now exist for creating graphics and desktop publishing for use with the Apple II family, the Macintosh, and the DOS machines. Desktop publishing software such as PageMaker can be used to craft page layouts of text and graphics, brochures, even multipage documents with many columns. Some are more sophisticated than others. State-of-the-art desktop publishing includes both sophisticated software and hardware such as laser printers. Users must develop skill and hone their creativity to employ these products properly.

The most commonly seen and used category of desktop publishing is that of specialty software programs that can create flyers, stationery, posters, banners, greeting cards, and puzzles and artwork for use with children. The best example is The Print Shop. The advantage of this type of software is that excellent-looking documents can be created quickly with little creativity. However, such programs have limited uses. The user punches in responses to a few questions or makes a few selections and out comes a nice looking flyer or banner. Specialty software also can be employed to create charts and graphs. Picture Perfect represents this class of software. It will create exquisite pie, vertical and horizontal bar, line/ area, bar/line, and other kinds of charts.

Another important class of software is the word processor. Only in the past few years have products formerly intended solely for basic text entry taken on the shape of desktop publishers. WordPerfect, one of the most popular and effective word processors around, is an excellent example. Users have access to a variety of tools, fonts, and other features. Integrated software programs such as Microsoft Works contain a word processor, a spreadsheet, a database management system, telecommunications, and graphics. In particular, Microsoft Works contains an excellent chart-making facility. Both of these programs are excellent for creating business reports containing statistics and charts.

In addition to complete desktop publishing packages and single-purpose specialty programs, there are painting and drawing programs that take originality and custom work to much greater limits. A drawing program provides many tools for creating artwork without the need to know much about drawing.

Most of the above-mentioned software packages can be enhanced with clip art. Since few people have the time or inclination to create much original artwork, clip art solves the problem by making predrawn art available for import into a graphics or desktop package. Clip art is associated with different coded formats: TIFF, PCX, EPS, etc., to ensure compatibility.

Graphics for different applications risk being stored in incompatible ways. Hence, their designation is given in the suffix of the file name. For instance, BIRD.WPG might be a file for a picture of a bird in WordPerfect format. There are many different types of such formats. They are referred to throughout the remainder of this book in descriptions of the software programs. Aside from making sure that the programs and clip art that is purchased are compatible, there are utility packages that will convert between formats. (See the section on Utilities.)

Fonts and typefaces are another important ingredient of creative publishing. A typeface is a term that covers a large range of type and all sizes of the same design type. For example, Courier New, in all point sizes, is one typeface. A font, on the other hand, is a more limited term used to describe only one size of a typeface. To put it succinctly, one typeface contains many fonts. A type family is a group of several similar typefaces, for example, Courier New, Courier New Bold, and Courier New Italic would be a type family. For many beginners, the fonts that come with the programs listed in this directory will be sufficient. As users become more sophisticated about type requirements, however, more variety will be desired. Add-on packages of several dozen fonts can be obtained at low cost and will provide most of the variety needed for library projects.

Selection of Software: A Simple System

Even though the variety of programs and accessories may be a bit bewildering to the beginner, on the whole it is a good thing. Something often forgotten is that the library profession encompasses a wide variety of people, talents, needs, and occupations. The needs for a legal library can be greatly different from those of a school library. The needs of a rural library are quite different from those of the Chicago Public Library. From the hundreds of available packages, there is something to meet almost everyone's needs.

Also important to keep in mind is that it is impossible to anticipate all needs at the beginning. So the average user will be adding utilities and other programs for the life of the computer.

Selecting software is a fact-finding mission. Tasks that will be required to make a selection include:

1. Learn about the software that is already installed on your microcomputer.
2. Make an inventory of tasks you wish to perform with the microcomputer (e.g., newsletter, flyer).
3. Use this volume to learn about the types of software that can perform the tasks you listed. Also, check vendors' catalogs or call vendors to determine system (hardware) requirements and other basic features. (A list of vendor names, addresses, and telephone numbers appears at the end of this book.)
4. Compare software titles through reviews in magazines, online sources, and software directories. Magazines and journals provide the most-recent news and reviews of software packages.
5. Ask around. See if libraries in your area are using any of the software you are interested in buying or which software they recommend.
6. Join a user group. Many grass-roots organizations exist for the sharing of information. Most are informal. Some exist through the mail, others through electronic means such as bulletin board systems and online services such as CompuServe.

Resources for Software Selection

Significant online resources can aid in hardware and software selection. Several DIALOG services, for example, are Business Software DataBase, Computer Database, Micro Software Directory, and Microcomputer Software Guide. Two excellent CD-ROM packages make it possible to search thousands of journal articles and vendor information quickly for reviews and product information. Computer Select ($995 per year through Computer Library, 20 Brace Road, Cherry Hill, NJ 08034; 609-354-5001) is published monthly. Many computer magazines are available full text, while many others are indexed with abstracts. Computer Demo ($199 per year, also from Computer Library) has more than 1,100 running demos of popular computer programs.

For years computer users have extolled the virtues of joining or organizing user groups. There are several types, any of which are useful. Any way in which people can communicate about a particular subject or interest can be termed a user group, or sometimes, special interest group (SIG). The most common is the community group that actually meets each month or so. This, of course, entails finding a place to meet, organizing the meeting, etc. While forming a users' group is a lot of work, actually meeting people, having demonstrations, and making contacts can be useful.

A second and easier way is to organize around a newsletter. With this format members seldom, if ever, meet, but they do have the opportunity to swap information via the newsletter and to write or call one another as the need arises. A directory of members' hardware and software can be published as well, adding further to each member's ability to find specific help.

A classic example of a users' group that has served the library community for years is the Apple Library User Group (ALUG). It has about 7,000 members, and the group holds meetings at library conferences. The big plus for this organization is its newsletter. Published by the Apple Library, the newsletter contains software and book reviews, news, first-hand accounts of library microcomputer adventures, and lots more.

Other ways to find people who share your interests include participating in online activities. By joining an online service you can have access to the thoughts and ideas of thousands of other people, even if not all of them are librarians. CompuServe, Delphi, and many other online services provide special interest group activity. Local bulletin boards can do the same thing and cost less to access. (For a list of bulletin boards in your area, see the *National Directory of Bulletin Board Systems* (Westport, Conn.: Meckler), an annual publication that lists some 10,000 bulletin boards around the United States and Canada and even has selected international listings.

What Will All of This Cost?

Because there are many levels of hardware and software from which to choose, the exact needs of the user will ultimately determine the final cost of a project. While it is possible to spend $35,000 and up for equipment and software, a typical cost for a library, single workstation is under $5,000.

Learning

There are lots of good ways to become proficient with microcomputers and the software that is installed on them. Basic familiarity with the computer is important before jumping into graphics production. Knowledge may be gained through using the tutorial programs that usually come with the microcomputer. On the other hand, some people can learn by just fiddling with the original instruction manual while sitting at the keyboard. In addition, many inexpensive manuals are available at computer stores.

Once basic skills have been mastered, there are several ways to attack the dual problems of making graphics software work and becoming good at designing a newsletter, flyer, or other product. The section on training programs in this book includes examples of additional products that teach important skills. There are videotapes that demonstrate programs and desktop skills. There are also classes available at local colleges, and agencies that teach microcomputer skills and graphics work. Furthermore, the bibliography at the end of this book lists materials that can be referred to on an ongoing basis for review, study, and examples of finished newsletters, etc.

Archives and Backups

Archives and backup copies are similar but not quite the same thing. Backing up material refers to current material. If you are working on a newsletter, it is important to keep a backup someplace until the project is finished. Some interval for updating the backup should be determined. A backup for material being stored on the hard drive should also be made periodically; otherwise, if your hard drive should crash, there will be no way to retrieve your work. Material may be archived once a project is finished. Each organization will have to assess how necessary it is to archive material. Some files, for example, scanned images of photographs, may be useful to keep for future projects. Most newsletter text will never be needed again.

Sources of Additional Information

Many books that are available can help the beginner develop sound principles for designing page layouts, including the following:

Burke, Clifford. *Type from the Desktop*. Chapel Hill, N.C.: Ventanna Press, 1990.
This excellent book gives good advice and illustrations for doing basic page layout. It focuses on design, style, and typeface management. However, the book does not deal with microcomputers.

Crawford, Walt. *Desktop Publishing for Librarians*. Boston, Mass.: G.K. Hall, 1990.
This outstanding volume has step-by-step procedures and advice for selecting the type and style of newsletter and other publications used by libraries.

Parker, Roger. *The Makeover Book*. Chapel Hill, N.C.: Ventanna Press, 1989.
An excellent source of publishing layout ideas, the book contains separate chapters on the preparation of newsletters, advertisements, brochures and flyers, reports and proposals, business correspondence, catalogs and booklets, and charts and graphs. It is generic and can be used with any graphics or desktop publishing package. The introductory chapter concentrates on acquainting the user with twenty-five problem areas, each posed as a question (e.g., Have you been consistent in your use of style? Did you overuse the tools of emphasis?).

Desktop Publishing Packages

The packages listed in this section are products specifically made for desktop publishing; they all make page layouts. Any one is an excellent choice for use by someone with specific public relations or graphics responsibilities.

Some of the many important things to look for in a package include ease of use, compatibility with other programs in use, cost, features, and suitability for the intended use.

Software must be selected on the basis of the type of computer available. In most cases, this will be either IBM compatible or Macintosh. Furthermore, because some programs gobble up large amounts of RAM and disk space, even the correct software for a type of computer may not work unless some expansion of the memory or other feature is made.

With regard to cost, it is possible to find something for every library's budget. Many systems sell for less than $100, while others are priced at nearly $1,000.

Low-end desktop publishers are generally useful for shorter documents such as brief newsletters, flyers, etc. Print Shop is an excellent example of this category. Such programs typically have a limited supply of fonts and clip art built in, though add-ons are usually available in a compatible format.

Mid-range desktop publishers will handle a wider range of projects. They also have more features available for handling text and graphics, such as the flow of text from page to page.

The high-end programs are often chosen by medium- to large-sized libraries, but much of their potential remains unused. High-end desktop publishers provide for creation of elaborate documents in color and features such as online communication. More advanced users of desktop publishing can use their program with a modem to send their compositions directly to a publisher. PageMaker is an example of a high-end product.

One other category includes The Writing Center. This product is intended as an educational package for schools.

Name: **Avagio Publishing System 2.0**
Program type: Low-end desktop publisher
Vendor: Unison World
Cost: $149.95
Hardware requirements: IBM compatible
Additional software available: AvaFonts 1, Art Gallery I & II, and Fonts & Borders
Description: Ten design templates make it possible to create sophisticated work within a short time. The system is useful for producing flyers, catalogs, newsletters, business reports, and other presentations. It is much easier to learn to use and manipulate than a more sophisticated system such as PageMaker. An unusual feature is the system's built-in font technology. It includes 30 typeface selections that may be scaled from 6 to 500 points without loss of detail. Fonts may also be compressed or expanded in single-point increments without the quality deteriorating. Text may be rotated 360 degrees and can be made to follow any curve or free-form line. Drawing capabilities include lines, circles, rectangles, triangles, arrows, stars up to 30 points in size, and polygons with up to 60 sides. Avagio will accept TIFF, PCX, EPS, UWI, PIC, and color PCX and TIFF formats. It is compatible with WordPerfect, Microsoft Word, and WordStar. This product is very high value for the money, with 150 graphics included in the package.
Review source: *Personal Publishing*, November 1990, 74.

Name: **DesignStudio**
Program type: High-end desktop publisher
Vendor: Letraset USA
Cost: $795
Hardware requirements: Macintosh
Description: Billed as an advanced version of Ready, Set, Go!, DesignStudio provides a full set of tools for creating page layouts including kerning and tracking. Productions may be any number of pages long. A block of text can be changed into any of fifteen shapes. Text will flow automatically within a block, column, or page. Creates WYSIWYG pages using either grids or guidelines.
Review source: *InfoWorld*, November 5, 1990, 76.

Name: **Express Publisher 2.0**
Program type: Low-end desktop publisher
Vendor: Power Up! Software Corp.

Cost:	$159.95
Hardware requirements:	IBM PC, XT, PS/2, AT with 640KB RAM minimum; hard disk drive; mouse; graphics adapter
Description:	Express Publisher is a low-end publishing package. Nevertheless, it can provide a relatively inexpensive way to create flyers and newsletters. It includes a large font library. Type can be adjusted from 6 to 144 points. Templates come preprogrammed into the system in the form of page styles. Special features include full page viewing, landscape printing, text wrap around graphic elements, headers and footers. The text wrap feature will mold the text to the graphic rather than to a box around the graphic (as is the case with many desktop publishing programs). Printer compatibility will utilize up to 300 dpi with a laser printer. Clip art is included. System, however, supports only black-and-white images, no grayscale or color. Files from word processors can generally be imported. Search and replace editing capability. Drawing elements permit circles, rotate, add shadows, etc. Style sheets make production much simpler than starting from scratch each time.
Review sources:	Henricks, Mark. *PC Computing*, November 1990, 80; *PC Computing*, May 1992, 352.

Name:	**Express Publisher for Windows**
Program type:	Low-end desktop publisher
Vendor:	Power Up! Software Corp.
Cost:	$249.95
Hardware requirements:	IBM compatible
Additional software needed:	Microsoft Windows
Description:	This is a version of Express Publisher that is specifically created to work with the popular Microsoft Windows operating environment. It is a versatile low-end desktop publishing program that provides numerous features. A set of predesigned templates makes it easy to choose one and enter text. Any part of a page can be "zoomed" for closer examination. The program includes 23 outline Adobe fonts in points from 4 to 720.
Review source:	*PC Computing*, May 1992, 354.

Name:	**FrameMaker 3.0**
Program type:	High-end desktop publisher
Vendor:	Frame Technology
Cost:	$795

Hardware requirements: Macintosh

Description: FrameMaker is an advanced WYSIWYG package that offers page layout, hypertext, equations editing, graphics, and word processing. Its math capabilities make it particularly suitable for business applications. Other features include 25 master pages per document, font sizes from 4 to 400 points (.001 increments), drawing tools, and the capability of mixing portrait and landscape pages within documents. It also allows users to rotate text and graphics, flip, and zoom and has special features for controlling long documents.

Review source: *MacWorld*, March 1992, 181.

Name: **Microsoft Publisher**

Program type: Medium-range desktop publisher

Vendor: Microsoft Corp.

Cost: $199

Hardware requirements: IBM compatible

Description: An inexpensive page layout program, Microsoft Publisher is relatively easy to get up and running. Many special features help in the production of newsletters, including built-in guides and automatic columns. An autoflow feature provides the ability to define a frame of any size, then import text into it. Frames can be resized and text adjusted accordingly. Excess text will flow to the next page. However, it does not allow contour wraparound. The system will import files in EPS, TIFF, and PCX formats. A set of "PageWizards" (templates) aids in designing publications with less difficulty than in higher-end systems. Fifteen fonts come with the system, and they may be stretched, shadowed, flipped, or arched. It is an outstanding value and can be up-and-running and producing useful work in only one short session.

Review source: *PC Computing*, May 1992, 358.

Name: **NewsMaster II**

Program type: Low-end desktop publisher

Vendor: Unison World Software

Cost: $59.95

Hardware requirements: IBM compatible; 512KB RAM minimum

Additional software available: Art Gallery I & II, from Unison Products, are compatible and provide additional clip art.

Description: NewsMaster is an entry level desktop publisher that is designed for limited but important functions. Text and graphics can be combined to form newsletters, charts, bulletins, menus, forms, etc. It can be used as an educational program in schools, by students doing the school paper, or by anyone producing a company newsletter. Documents may have from one to ten columns per page. More than 275 graphic images and 30 fonts come with the system. Vertical, horizontal, and box lines can be added and filled with any one of thirty patterns. A WYSIWYG product is created on screen prior to printing out in different print modes (draft, high quality, etc.). Four different page views and six levels of zoom are available for previewing.

Name: **PageMaker**
Program type: High-end page layout program
Vendor: Aldus Corp.
Cost: $795
Hardware requirements: IBM compatible
Description: PageMaker is perhaps the best known and most important of all the page layout programs for the IBM-compatible series of computers. It offers a full range of options and features for virtually any type of advanced layout work. It has word processing and spell checking features. Drawing elements, such as lines, boxes, etc., are available. As an overall page program, it is more user friendly than many other systems. The program is excellent for long documents, and the system will create an index and table of contents. See the reference in *MacWorld* (following) for an excellent point-by-point comparison with Quark-XPress, the leading contender.
Review source: *MacWorld*, February 1991, 148.

Name: **PagePlus**
Program type: Medium-range desktop publisher
Vendor: Serif
Cost: $129
Hardware requirements: IBM compatible
Description: Its ease of use and moderate cost are two good points about this program. Another is that, as work progresses, the system automatically saves material every few minutes. The user can "revert" to a previously saved ver-

sion, if necessary. Formatting is stripped away from imported text. The system has poor word-processing features, so most users will want to use a full-featured word-processing package for creating text. There are many features missing, such as picture preview and stylesheets. The program includes more than 100 clip art images (PCX format) and 71 fonts. Clip art groups are office, technology, leisure, general, people, and dingbats.

Review source: *PC Computing*, May 1992, 360.

Name: **Personal Press**
Program type: Medium-range desktop publishing
Vendor: Aldus Corp.
Cost: $109
Hardware requirements: Macintosh
Description: This versatile desktop publisher offers a host of features. Page layout can be automated in some ways, including with the use of templates for creating greeting cards, newsletters, brochures, flyers, memos, etc. Templates can be easily adjusted and offer a variety of easy-to-use variations in each. Other features include a full-featured word processor with excellent speller, automatic adjustment of copy on page, gray-scale shades, text wrap around any shape, online help available, and many more. Thumbnail sketch (AutoCreate) previews a document as it is being created and changed. The program is fully capable of special features such as pulled quotes and bulleted text.

Name: **Personal Publisher**
Program type: Medium-range desktop publisher
Vendor: Expert Software
Cost: $14.95
Hardware requirements: IBM compatible
Description: It is extremely simple and easy to use this program for generating low-end products. Users can create awards, ads, flyers, and even a newsletter.

Name: **PFS: First Publisher 3.0**
Program type: Medium-range desktop publisher
Vendor: Spinnaker Software Corp.
Cost: $149

Hardware requirements:	IBM compatible; 512KB RAM minimum; 2MB disk space
Additional software available:	PFS: Font Library 3.0 ($74.95; contains 21 typefaces and 70 fonts), PFS: Recreation Gallery 3.0 ($74.95; contains an excellent collection of 600 drawn images, including hobbies, sports, pets, etc.), Works of Art Laser Art—Business Selection ($99.95; 125 business images for use with PostScript printers), Works of Art Laser Fonts—Volume 1 ($99.95; contains PostScript fonts Celeste, Circus, Old German, Oxford, and Modern).
Description:	The PFS desktop publishing package is designed for quick, easy page layouts. It comes with a number of easy-to-use features and contains page templates and a gallery of art. PFS can be used to create newsletters, flyers, brochures, cards, etc. Its many add-on packages give excellent support to this package.

Name:	**PFS: First Publisher for Windows 1.1**
Program type:	Medium-range desktop publisher
Vendor:	Spinnaker Software Corp.
Cost:	$149
Hardware requirements:	IBM compatible; 2MB RAM minimum; 3.5MB disk space
Additional software needed:	Windows 3.x
Additional software available:	PFS: Font Library 3.0 ($74.95; contains 21 typefaces and 70 fonts), PFS: Recreation Gallery 3.0 ($74.95; contains an excellent collection of 600 drawn images, including hobbies, sports, pets, etc.), Works of Art Laser Art—Business Selection ($99.95; 125 business images for use with PostScript printers), Works of Art Laser Fonts—Volume 1 ($99.95; contains PostScript fonts Celeste, Circus, Old German, Oxford, and Modern).
Description:	The PFS desktop publishing package is designed for quick, easy page layouts. It comes with a number of easy-to-use features and contains page templates and a gallery of art. PFS can be used to create newsletters, flyers, brochures, cards, etc. Its many add-on packages give excellent support to this package.

Name:	**Print Shop Deluxe**
Program type:	Low-end desktop publisher
Vendor:	Broderbund Software, Inc.
Cost:	$79.95

Hardware requirements: IBM compatible; 2MB RAM minimum; 1.5MB disk space

Additional software available: By adding the Sampler Edition, School or Business, or Party Edition, many additional graphics can be added. See Clip Art section of this book for collections for Print Shop.

Description: This is perhaps the most widely used general graphics program in existence: more than three million copies of its various versions have been sold. It was a forerunner of the current desktop publishing enthusiasm. Many add-ons now exist that greatly enhance the original product. This new edition includes major improvements over the old. The system contains new tools and capabilities. Users can create a multitude of finished products; Print Shop Deluxe is a very structured and menu-driven system. Users begin with the main menu and make selections regarding type of document and its layout.

Perhaps the thing that has made this program so very popular for so many years is its ease of use. With absolutely no experience, a first-time user can create sophisticated posters, flyers, letterheads, banners, and much more. While it is certainly not a page layout program, it does make it very easy to balance and custom create work.

The new version of the system allows for greater flexibility than the old version and produces labels, business cards, ads, games, tickets, calendars, and wrapping papers. Print Shop Deluxe also provides many ready-made borders, alignment of text, etc. Graphics can now be placed anywhere on a page.

Review source: *Newsbytes*, August 28, 1992.

Additional source of information: Schenck, Mary, and Randi Benton. *The Official New Print Shop Handbook*. New York: Bantam, 1990.

Name: **Print Shop Deluxe for Windows**

Program type: Low-end desktop publisher

Vendor: Broderbund Software, Inc.

Cost: $79.95

Hardware requirements: IBM compatible; 2MB RAM minimum; 1.5MB disk space

Additional software available: By adding the Sampler Edition, School or Business, or Party Edition, many additional graphics can be added.

See Clip Art section of this book for collections for Print Shop.

Description: This is perhaps one of the most widely used general graphics programs in existence: more than three million copies of its various versions have been sold. It was a forerunner of the current desktop publishing enthusiasm. Many add-ons now exist that greatly enhance the original product. This new edition includes major improvements over the old. The system contains new tools and capabilities. Users can create a multitude of finished products; Print Shop Deluxe for Windows is a very structured and menu-driven system. Users begin with the main menu and make selections regarding type of document and its layout.

Perhaps the thing that has made this program so very popular for so many years is its ease of use. With absolutely no experience, a first-time user can create sophisticated posters, flyers, letterheads, banners, and much more. While it is certainly not a page layout program, it does make it very easy to balance and custom create work.

The new version of the system allows for greater flexibility than the old version and produces labels, business cards, ads, games, tickets, calendars, and wrapping papers. Print Shop Deluxe for Windows also provides many ready-made borders, alignment of text, etc. Graphics can now be placed anywhere on a page.

Review source: *Newsbytes*, August 28, 1992.

Additional source of information: Schenck, Mary, and Randi Benton. *The Official New Print Shop Handbook*. New York: Bantam, 1990.

Name: **Publish It! 3.0**

Program type: Medium-range desktop publisher

Vendor: TimeWorks, Inc.

Cost: $149.95

Hardware requirements: IBM compatible; 640KB RAM minimum; 1.5MB disk space

Additional software available: Publish It! Easy 3.0 and Publish It! for Windows 3.0

Description: Publish It! is a full desktop publishing program that contains many features. It includes a word-processing mode, page layout, and graphics. The program makes full use of pull-down menus, scroll bars, dialogue boxes, and icons and is a simple system to use. It uses 9- to 72-point type, including bold, italic, and underlined, outlined, shadow, and super- or subscript. Some templates to aid speedy production are also included. It is, unfortunately, a slow program and lacks many of the features expected of packages available for other computers. It comes in a variety of versions for different users (i.e., see Publish It Lite!, following).

Review sources: *PC Magazine*, February 27, 1990, 147; *PC Computing*, May 1992, 364.

Name: **Publish It Lite! 1.0**
Program type: Low-end desktop publisher
Vendor: TimeWorks, Inc.
Cost: $59.95
Hardware requirements: IBM compatible
Description: Scaled-down and less-expensive version of Publish It! described previously.

Name: **QuarkXPress 3.2**
Program type: Low-end desktop publisher
Vendor: Quark, Inc.
Cost: $195
Hardware requirements: Macintosh
Description: The program offers considerable features and improvements over previous versions. A major problem with this system has been the difficulty of learning to use it. This has been partially remedied by the addition of a new interactive menu window. The system provides for master pages and document pages. Special features such as the ability to flow text within a shape can make for interesting and creative documents. A full range of color features permit advanced magazine and artwork production. The Library feature is used to store up to 2,000 items or item groups for later use in documents. Small miniatures or icons are dragged between the document and the library as needed.
Review source: *MacWorld*, July 1992, 199.

Name: **QuarkXPress 3.2 for Windows**
Program type: Medium-range desktop publisher
Vendor: Quark, Inc.
Cost: $895

Hardware requirements:	IBM compatible; 4MB RAM minimum; 15MB disk space
Additional software needed:	Windows 3.x
Description:	This very recent introduction to the market is similar to the program previously listed, but functions within the Windows operating environment. It takes advantage of pull-down menus, the mouse, and icons.
Review source:	*PC Magazine*, December 8, 1992, 37.

Name:	**Ready, Set, Go 5.0**
Program type:	Low-end desktop publisher
Vendor:	Manhattan Graphics Corp.
Cost:	$395
Hardware requirements:	Macintosh; 2MB RAM minimum
Description:	Ready, Set, Go is an excellent program for page design. It contains a full range of tools and features. The system contains a word processor and is compatible with Microsoft Works, Word, WordPerfect, WriteNow, Mac-Write, ASCII, TIFF, RIFF, EPSF, PICT, and MacPaint files.

Working with Ready, Set, Go is not difficult. The user can cut and paste between documents. Documents may have unlimited pages or be spread across two pages. The grid system makes for easy placement of graphics and text. Pages can be displayed with thumbnail views on the monitor. Changes such as deleting and moving pages in the thumbnails result in the same changes in the document.

Rotation of individual text or graphics can be made in increments of one-tenth of one degree in any direction. Rectangles can be created and filled with any of fifty-two patterns. Special effects include a gray-map editor for brightness, darkness, and clarity. Kerning and other typographic options included: font, size, alignment, hyphenation.

Add-on modules, called annexes, permit considerable improvement or change in the program's performance. Some of these include international annexes. These are add-ons that allow the program to work in any combination of eighteen foreign languages: French, German, Italian, Finnish, Icelandic, etc.

Other features include a glossary (library) of easy to find page elements for quick retrieval. Greeking, a way to judge a layout without having the actual text, is supported. Objects on screen may be locked so that they are not altered by accident. Ready, Set, Go has a wide variety of additional features available for control of the page, printing, and working.

Name:	**Rubicon Desktop Publisher**
Program type:	Low-end desktop publisher
Vendor:	Software Labs (shareware)
Cost:	$7.38 (shareware)
Hardware requirements:	IBM compatible
Additional software needed:	Word processor that saves file as ASCII text
Description:	This program is one of the few shareware programs that provides full desktop capabilities to users with marginal hardware. The most important distinction between this package and others is that this program only processes text—no graphics. It does, however, support a LaserJet or PostScript printer and a 9- or 24-pin dot matrix printer.

Name:	**Ventura Database Publisher DOS edition**
Program type:	High-end desktop publisher for use with a database
Vendor:	Ventura Software, Inc.
Cost:	$295
Hardware requirements:	IBM compatible
Description:	Information in DBS, SDF, CDF, or ASCII formats can be captured by this publishing program and converted to formatted documents. This program makes data from spreadsheets and database systems much easier to work with than was previously possible with just the Ventura Publisher. Data files can be transformed into charts, directories, catalogs, etc. Special features include a Tables mode, which will create multiple tables from the same data, and layout changes, such as tint background, etc.
Review source:	*PC Magazine*, February 11, 1992, 49.

Name:	**Ventura Publisher 3.0**
Program type:	High-end desktop publisher
Vendor:	Ventura Software, Inc.
Cost:	$795
Hardware requirements:	IBM compatible; 640KB RAM minimum; 10MB disk space
Description:	GEM operating system now provides powerful Windows-like operation of the Ventura Publisher, making it

easy to shift from function to function. The program has the ability to easily create documents hundreds of pages in length, including books. Tables, pages, and illustrations are cross-referenced automatically so that changes in one result in correct page changes in the others.

Review source: *PC Computing*, October 1990, 54.

Name: **Ventura Publisher Macintosh Edition 3.2**
Program type: High-end desktop publisher
Vendor: Ventura Software, Inc.
Cost: $795
Hardware requirements: Macintosh; 2MB RAM minimum; 20MB disk space
Description: Similar to previous product but for the Macintosh work environment.

Name: **Ventura Publisher, Windows Edition 4.1**
Program type: High-end desktop publisher
Vendor: Ventura Software, Inc.
Cost: $795
Hardware requirements: IBM compatible
Additional software needed: Windows
Description: This Ventura Publisher edition is specially programmed for use with the Windows operating environment. It includes word processing with spell check, graphics capability, and much more. Data can be exchanged with other Windows software, including CorelDraw!, Excel, PowerPoint, and others. The system also supports Pantone color.
Review source: *PC Computing*, January 1992, 108.

Specialty Graphics Products

There are now many easy-to-use, single- (or few) function, low-cost graphics packages available. These are the very low end of the graphics industry. These products will do many things, though they are not in any sense page layout programs or paint programs.

Examples of such packages are plentiful. BannerMania, a popular program, creates outstanding banners within seconds using various fonts, graphics, and special effects. Other similar programs even specialize in one subarea, such as flyer production. Certificate Maker makes it easy to create award and certificate shells or patterns. After these are filled in, the computer produces the custom product in a couple of minutes. Other specialty programs in the following list create fax cover sheets, greeting cards, handbooks, charts, and much more.

Name:	**Award Maker Plus**
Program type:	Certificate maker
Vendor:	Baudville Computer Products
Cost:	$59.95 (Apple II family); $49.95 (IBM and Macintosh).
Hardware requirements:	Apple II, IBM compatibles, Macintosh
Additional software available:	Add-on for sports or education $29.95; cartoons add-on $19.95; laser edition $199
Description:	This classy program makes awards similar in scope to Certificate Maker, described later. Tremendous variety is available. A selection of four typefaces (Old English, Script Italic, Book Serif, and Modern) provides for highly formal-looking certificates. Ten borders can be used to dress up documents. Special editions of add-ons are available for sports, education, and cartoons. The education and sports add-ons use four additional fonts (Casual, Old West, Typewriter, and Pen Script). Each also includes approximately eight new borders appropriate for the subject. The cartoon add-on provides many additional cartoons for use with any certificate. Certificates look very professional.

Name:	**BannerMania**
Program type:	Banner maker
Vendor:	Broderbund Software, Inc.
Cost:	$34.95 (IBM); $59.95 (Macintosh)
Hardware requirements:	IBM PC; Macintosh
Description:	This is the best program yet for the production of banners of all types. While there are variations in the Macintosh and the IBM versions of this program, they both have preprogrammed designs, a selection of nineteen fonts, many shapes, and special effects. Most of these can be used together as needed to make a wide variety of banners and posters available. The program can create one- or two-line messages in different colors and patterns on a banner. Special effects include three-dimensional lettering. Additional fonts may be imported from the Adobe Systems type libraries. No clip art is included; however, it does have a few special symbols that add life to banners, such as hearts, pointing fingers, etc. The strength of the program lies in its ability to manipulate the text into different special effects and shapes.
Review source:	*MacUser*, August 1992, 87.

Name:	**Banner Printer**
Program type:	Banner maker
Vendor:	Public Domain Exchange
Cost:	$9.95 (shareware)
Hardware requirements:	Apple II
Description:	Banner Printer is a limited but useful and inexpensive program that makes banners up to five lines in length in upper- and lower-case letters.

Name:	**Certificate Maker**
Program type:	Certificate maker
Vendor:	Spinnaker Software Corp.
Cost:	$44.95
Hardware requirements:	IBM compatible; Macintosh; 800KB RAM minimum
Additional software available:	Certificate Library Volume 1, which contains more than 100 additional certificate styles, 24 borders, and 72 stickers.
Description:	Simple and easy to use, the program provides users with many options for creating certificates for use with reading programs, school work, awards, etc.

Name:	**ChartBuilder for Visual Basic 2.0**
Program type:	Graph maker
Vendor:	Pinnacle Publishing Inc.
Cost:	$149
Hardware requirements:	IBM compatible; 1MB RAM minimum; 1MB hard disk space
Additional software needed:	Microsoft Visual Basic; Windows 3.x
Description:	Owners of Microsoft's Visual Basic may use this program to add graphing capabilities. Nine chart types are included: bar, line, polar, area, pie charts, log/linear, scatter, Gantt and high-low-close charts.
Review source:	*Data Based Advisor*, November 1992, 118.

Name:	**DeltaGraph Professional 2.01**
Program type:	Chart and graph maker
Vendor:	DeltaPoint, Inc.
Cost:	$199
Hardware requirements:	Macintosh; 2MB RAM minimum; 4MB disk space
Description:	This high-quality, graph-production system will make excellent text charts and custom chart libraries with color options. There is a built-in slide show capability. The newest version features 40 different types of charts with 300 features and enhancements. PostScript drawing tools include Bezier curves and arcs, lines, etc.

Name:	**DeltaGraph Professional for Windows 2.0**
Program type:	Chart and graph maker
Vendor:	DeltaPoint, Inc.
Cost:	$495
Hardware requirements:	IBM compatible; 2MB RAM minimum; 7MB disk space
Additional software needed:	Windows 3.x
Description:	DeltaGraph, a high-quality graph-production system, will make excellent text charts and custom chart libraries with color options. There is a built-in slide show capability. The newest version features 40 different types of charts with 300 features and enhancements. PostScript drawing tools include Bezier curves and arcs, lines, etc.

Name:	**EasyFlow 7.0**
Program type:	Chart maker
Vendor:	Haven Tree Software Limited
Cost:	$280 (IBM compatible version); $339 (Macintosh version)

Hardware requirements: IBM compatible; 512KB RAM minimum; 1MB hard disk space

Description: The program automates the creation of organization and flow charts and data-flow diagrams to any size. Larger charts than a printer can handle are printed in smaller sections, page by page, for combining into a larger chart. It contains 130 pages of documentation and 150 screens of context-sensitive online help.

Name: **Fast Forms**
Program type: Form maker
Vendor: Power Up! Software Corp.
Cost: $179.95
Hardware requirements: Macintosh
Description: Using Fast Forms anyone can create any type of sophisticated form. The use of gray scale, hair lines, reversed type, and other features can generate custom forms for any purpose. The finished product can be printed out or filled in from within the program. The package also has a spreadsheet function that will automatically perform calculations.

Name: **FaxBuilder**
Program type: Fax cover sheet maker
Vendor: Unison World Software
Cost: $49.95
Hardware requirements: IBM compatible; 640KB RAM minimum; CGA video adapter
Description: This stand-alone program creates custom cover sheets for fax transmissions using 25 pieces of clip art, 4 fonts, and 20 templates. Output may be seen as WYSIWYG prior to printing. The program's database function saves information on people receiving faxes so that it can be used again without having to reenter it.

Name: **FaxMania Business Fax Cover Sheets**
Program type: Fax cover sheet maker
Vendor: T/Maker Co.
Cost: $49.95
Hardware requirements: IBM compatible; Macintosh
Description: FaxMania creates impressive fax cover sheets to go with your faxes. The highly versatile program includes clip art suitable for business occasions and special events and for

fun (FAX from Hell, Rumor Fax, etc.). Eighty cover sheets are included, all of which can be customized.

Review source: *PC World*, September 1992, 70.

Name: **FaxMania for Windows**
Program: Fax cover sheet maker
Vendor: T/Maker Co.
Cost: $49.95
Hardware requirements: IBM compatible
Additional software needed: Windows 3.x
Description: This program offers eighty fax cover sheets for business and special occasions. It is the same as the previous product except that it uses the Windows operating environment.

Review source: *PC Computing*, August 1992, 70.

Name: **FormTool Gold 3.0**
Program type: Form maker
Vendor: BLOCPublishing Corp.
Cost: $99.95
Hardware requirements: IBM compatible; 256KB RAM minimum
Description: An excellent tool, this program creates many types of forms. Automatic drawing tools allow for creating perfect boxes and make drawing forms very easy. It also contains a FormTool Encyclopedia of tips and techniques for form design and dozens of templates for immediate use. Included are forms for invoices, calendars, budgets, fax cover sheets, work orders, purchase orders, etc. Products are created in a WYSIWYG format. Highly flexible, FormTool will create form boxes with rounded corners, if desired. Text may be added anywhere on forms with word wrap, as captions, centered, and with many word-processing features. The system will use up to 72-point type and any available font. It allows variable line widths and dotted lines and has special characters, such as math and science symbols, ballot boxes, etc. Forms may be printed sideways, too. Boxes, lines, and grids may all be moved very easily. A file manager keeps track of forms and allows for easy moving, copying, archiving, or deletion of any form.

Name: **Handbook**
Program type: Handbook maker
Vendor: Software Labs

Cost: $3.69 (shareware)

Hardware requirements: IBM compatible (supports Epson FX, ProPrinter, and LaserJet printers)

Description: As its name suggests, this is a limited though useful program for creating a single product: a handbook. Considerable customizing allowed. It uses 8.5 by 11 inch paper, four pages per side. The finished product has centered headings and alphabetic index pages.

Name: **Intouch 2.0**

Program type: Name and address system

Vendor: Advanced Software, Inc.

Cost: $69.95

Hardware requirements: Macintosh; 1MB RAM minimum; 500KB disk space; modem (optional)

Additional software needed: Microsoft Word

Description: The Intouch system maintains personal name and address lists using Microsoft Word. It prints a single envelope from within Word or an entire label set. Unlimited names, addresses, phone numbers, notes can be captured. It even dials telephone numbers.

Name: **Let's Make Calendars and Stationery**

Program type: Calendar and stationery maker

Vendor: Melody Hall

Cost: $9.95

Hardware requirements: IBM compatibles

Description: Calendars and stationery are very easy to construct with this program. If used for public access, patrons should have little trouble creating their own productions. Staff can use it, too.

Name: **Let's Make Greeting Cards**

Program type: Greeting-card maker

Vendor: Melody Hall

Cost: $9.95

Hardware requirements: IBM compatible

Description: As its name implies, this single-function program provides various possibilities for creating greeting cards. It could be used as a public access program with little instruction or help.

Name: **Let's Make Signs & Banners**
Program type: Sign and banner maker
Vendor: Melody Hall
Cost: $9.95
Hardware requirements: IBM compatible
Description: This simple program creates a variety of signs and banners but not much else. The price is right, however.

Name: **Letterhead Generator**
Program type: Letterhead maker
Vendor: Software Labs
Cost: $3.69 (shareware)
Hardware requirements: IBM compatible
Description: The major function of this program is to create letterheads with logos at the top or side of stationery. It also produces index cards and custom envelopes.

Name: **Library Magic**
Program type: Bookmark, certificate, and form generator
Vendor: McCarthy-McCormack, Inc.
Cost: $49.95
Hardware requirements: Apple II series
Description: This self-contained and easy-to-use program offers a variety of projects of interest to school and library professionals. While much of what it offers is easily found elsewhere, some items, such as thirty-two varieties of bookmarks and a bookworm that grows and grows, are worthwhile for school librarians and media center specialists. It also makes book reservation forms, loan requests, library cards, overdue notices, passes, and twenty different kinds of awards.

Name: **Looney Tunes Print Kit**
Program type: Print kit with cartoon characters
Vendor: Hi Tech Expressions
Cost: $14.95
Hardware requirements: IBM compatible
Description: Add cartoon characters to your flyers, bookmarks, and signs with this kit. It comes complete for simple jobs with 7 fonts, 20 borders, and 60 Looney Tunes characters in high resolution outline, including Daffy Duck, Bugs Bunny, Wile E. Coyote, Sylvester and Tweety, Elmer Fudd, Yosemite Sam, and many more.

Name: **Newsroom and Newsroom Pro**
Program type: Newsletter maker
Vendor: Spinnaker Software Corp.
Cost: $20 (Newsroom); $40 (Newsroom Pro)
Hardware requirements: IBM compatible; 256KB RAM minimum
Description: As the title suggests, this program has one function: newsletter production. Typical of most programs that do only one basic thing, this one has many limitations, but the trade-off is that it is much easier to use than other programs of its type. Newsroom comes with more than 600 pieces of clip art and Newsroom Pro with more than 2,000.

Name: **OrgPlus Advanced 6.0**
Program type: Organization chart maker
Vendor: Banner Blue Software, Inc.
Cost: $99
Hardware requirements: IBM compatible; Macintosh; 1MB RAM minimum; 1MB disk space
Description: This is the emperor of organizational chart programs. Users can create up to twenty different chart styles and combinations. Additional variations are provided for twelve border styles, line styles (solid, dotted, dashed), eight line thicknesses, and eight staff and assistant styles. Once a basic chart has been created, it may be saved, then edited quickly and easily by department, style, or text. The overall capacity of this system cannot be beat either, with 32,000 boxes allowed per chart, 50 levels, and an overall size of 10 by 10 feet. Within the Windows environment, there may be up to eight charts open at any one time. Customized clip art can be imported into the system as can any tab- or comma-delimited ASCII file.

Although not for every library, it can prove a valuable organizational tool for large organizations with many departments and employees.
Review sources: *MacWorld*, May 1991, 187; *PC Magazine*, December 17, 1991, 363.

Name: **OrgPlus for Windows 1.0**
Program type: Organization chart maker
Vendor: Banner Blue Software, Inc.
Cost: $199

Hardware requirements: IBM compatible; 1MB RAM minimum; 1.5MB disk space

Additional software needed: Windows 3.x

Description: Although similar to the DOS version, previously described, this version has more features and is more convenient to use. It includes 20 predefined styles and supports spaces for up to 32,000 positions with titles. The system is also more flexible than the DOS version.

Review source: *PC Magazine*, April 28, 1992, 48.

Name: **Page Director**

Program type: Page element manager

Vendor: Managing Editor Software

Cost: $895

Hardware requirements: Macintosh

Description: For the folks handling large publications or frequent installments that require the use and tracking of many different elements, this program will simplify life. The program has two parts: The Page Director application lets the user create a dummy publication. The Gather command will assist in reading and measuring text and graphic files to make the actual publication.

Review source: *MacWorld*, May 1991, 170.

Name: **Perfect Labels**

Program type: Label maker

Vendor: Expert Software

Cost: $14.95

Hardware requirements: IBM compatible

Description: The program creates and uses mailing labels from original or imported files.

Name: **PerForm Pro**

Program type: Form maker

Vendor: Delrina Technology, Inc.

Cost: $495

Hardware requirements: IBM compatible

Additional software needed: Windows

Description: This popular product comes with more than 100 sample forms for helping users design and generate a wide variety of documents: appraisal forms, personnel files, expense reports, etc. It includes security features to prevent unauthorized access to files. A special feature permits the use of electronic signatures in forms. Advanced features will automatically calculate and fill in dates, annuity values, and much more.

Review source: *PC Computing*, December 1990, 82.

Name: **Picture Label**
Program type: Label maker
Vendor: Software Labs
Cost: $3.69 (shareware; purchasers will initially receive disk that only prints two labels at one time; upon registering with shareware owner [$10] new disk will print 5,000)
Hardware requirements: IBM compatible
Description: This stand-alone address label program prints up to five lines and logos taken from any Print Shop or PrintMaster clip art.

Name: **Picture Perfect 4.1**
Program type: Graph and chart maker
Vendor: Computer Support Corp.
Cost: $295
Hardware requirements: IBM compatible; 640KB RAM minimum; 1.5MB disk space
Description: An excellent program for creating graphs and charts from raw data, Picture Perfect comes with thirteen typefaces for displaying data. A variety of charts can be produced: line/area, bar/line, and pie. These can be highlighted with shading. Pie charts can also be exploded. The system will accept some external data formats: ASCII row/column (fixed), ASCII row/column (variable).

Name: **PosterWorks 3.0**
Program type: Banner maker
Vendor: S. H. Pierce & Co.
Cost: $395
Hardware requirements: Macintosh; 2MB RAM minimum; 20MB disk space
Description: PosterWorks is a highly sophisticated poster program that can import scanned images from Mac and DOS TIFF files. In addition, it will create titled posters, billboards, and other displays. It is possible to create enormous posters, up to 10,000 square feet. Work is done on a blank pasteboard. If the poster is to be larger than one page, then initial layout shows tiled sheets that can be zoomed individually for work with rulers, tool palette, etc. Text,

illustrations, and scanned images all can be imported into the pasteboard for editing. The system is compatible with FreeHand, PageMaker, QuarkXPress, and CorelDraw. Pages from these programs can be imported into PosterWorks and edited as required. Tools available include: scaling, stretching, and cropping. Objects are layered, not merged, so each element can be individually reselected for editing. PosterWorks is fully compatible with EPS files and TIFF and Scitext CT formats. It also is compatible with Adobe and non-Adobe PostScript interpreters, Adobe Type Manager.

Review source: *PC Week*, August 31, 1992, 38.

Name: **Print Magic** (sold with Studio of Greetings, described later)

Program type: Sign and banner maker

Vendor: Epyx, Inc.

Cost: $39.95

Hardware requirements: IBM compatible, CGA graphics required; 384KB RAM

Description: Print Magic is an easy-to-use program for making certificates, banners, stationery, flyers, and greeting cards. The package includes more than 100 clip art graphics such as borders.

Name: **PrintMaster Gold**

Program type: Specialty program

Vendor: Unison World Software

Cost: $79.95

Hardware requirements: IBM compatible

Additional software available: Works with Art Gallery I & II, Fonts & Borders, Fantasy and American History. (All are enhancements for this product by Unison World.) PrintMaster Plus, an earlier version, is still available and described next.

Description: An easy-to-use program, PrintMaster Gold is similar in some ways to Print Shop. Users can create stationery, greeting cards, invitations, posters, banners, report covers, certificates, menus, announcements, and other forms with relative ease. A graphics editor makes custom changes in designs possible. It has 100 scalable outline graphics with special effects. The program works with fonts from Avagio, PrintMaster Plus, and both the old and new versions of the Print Shop. It supports PCX, TIFF, color PCX and TIFF, GIF and Windows BMP formats. It also includes a calendar (month, week, work week, weekends, extended weekends, and customized) that can be used with graphics; multiple lines of text can be inserted for each day. Color calendars also can be printed.

Name:	**PrintMaster Plus 2.0**
Program type:	Specialty program
Vendor:	Unison World Software
Cost:	$39.95
Hardware requirements:	IBM compatible; 256KB RAM minimum; 3MB disk space
Description:	While not as impressive as PrintMaster Gold, this program provides many excellent features for creating banners, posters, invitations, and other simple projects. It includes 122 graphic images, 10 fonts, and 11 borders for a good variety of design elements from which to choose.

Name:	**PrintPartner**
Program type:	Sign and banner maker
Vendor:	Software Labs
Cost:	$3.69 (shareware)
Hardware requirements:	IBM compatible (color graphics required), dot matrix or HP-LaserJet-compatible laser printer.
Description:	Similar in concept and execution to Print Shop and PrintMaster, PrintPartner contains 75 pieces of graphics. The program design allows for one or two graphics in any of three sizes on each finished product. Eleven fonts are included. Fifteen lines of text are allowed on signs, left- or right-justified or centered. A monthly calendar can be generated for any period from 1980 to 2098 in different fonts. Save, reload, and edit features are available. The system will also use PrintMaster clip art collections.

Name:	**Sign & Banner Maker**
Program type:	Sign and banner maker
Vendor:	Software Labs
Cost:	$3.69 (shareware)
Hardware requirements:	IBM compatible
Description:	As its name implies, this product contains five separate programs for making signs and banners. It is an inexpensive way for beginners to try out a system for creating graphics because it allows for control over many individ-

ual elements including size, spacing, shading, and printing horizontally or vertically.

Name:	**Smart Art I, II, III, and IV**
Program type:	Special effects for text
Vendor:	Adobe Systems, Inc.
Cost:	$149 per volume
Hardware requirements:	Macintosh; 1MB RAM minimum
Description:	This desk accessory series offers a variety of special effects for use with Mac applications. It creates enhanced EPS files. Volume 1 adds special effects to text; Volume 2 adds special effects to layouts, including bomb bursts, stars, arrows, spirals, etc.; Volume 3's additional text effects include slanted type, drop caps, double borders, etc.; Volume 4 contains headline fonts and special effects such as Block Letter, Brick, Diffuse, Multistar, Ribbon, etc.

Name:	**Statistica/Mac and Statistica/DOS**
Program type:	Statistical data analysis
Vendor:	StatSoft
Cost:	$495 (Macintosh); $795 (DOS version)
Hardware requirements:	Macintosh; IBM compatible
Description:	This is truly a high-end graphics/charting and database system, probably far in excess of anything most librarians will ever need for getting out their monthly or annual reports or budget. However, should the urge strike to perform log-linear analysis, survival-and-failure time analysis, and quality-control charts, this is definitely the program to choose. On a more serious note, the program does perform many other types of visualization of data that can be useful for librarians. This program provides outstanding data analysis. Hundreds of different charts, including color, are available. More than 1,000 presentation-quality graphics are available, and these can be modified onscreen.

Among its many features are exploratory techniques, descriptive statistics, frequency tables, large selection of nonparametric extended diagnostics, logit/probit transformations, general implementation of ANOVA/ANCOVA/MANOVA/MANCOVA, ganomical analysis statistics, and much more. Both 2-D and 3-D graphs supported, with 3-D showing real-time rotation facilities. This will make your monthly statistics look like they were produced by NASA.

The database component also contains a powerful programming language for more-sophisticated users.

Name:	**Studio of Greetings!** (includes Print Magic)
Program type:	Greeting Card Maker
Vendor:	Epyx, Inc.
Cost:	$69.95
Hardware requirements:	IBM compatible; Macintosh
Description:	This ready-made program creates an impressively wide variety of greeting cards. Included are more than 400 graphics and 400 accent images. Images are bit-mapped. The program is compatible with Print Shop, Windows, and PC Paintbrush. More than 700 greeting card ideas are presented in the *Design Ideas Book*.

Name:	**Super Sign Maker**
Program type:	Sign and banner maker
Vendor:	Sunburst Communications, Inc.
Cost:	$75 single disk, or $225 for lab pack of ten (Apple II, either 3.5 or 5.25 inch); $65 single disk, or $195 lab pack of ten (IBM compatible); $300 for Apple Talk Network.
Hardware requirements:	Apple II series; IBM compatible
Additional software available:	The Super Sign Maker Library Disk #2 contains seventeen additional patterned borders and more than thirty new pictures.
Description:	This program creates banners, signs, and handouts using a selection of borders, type styles, and letter heights of ½ inch to 8 inches. Letters can be produced in outline form as something for younger students to color. Productions can be previewed onscreen prior to actually printing.

Name:	**Top Honors**
Program type:	Certificate maker
Vendor:	Spinnaker Software Corp.
Cost:	$99.95
Hardware requirements:	Macintosh
Description:	Top Honors is an outstanding certificate program that supplies 24 high-resolution borders, 7 high-resolution seals, date line, up to 4 signature lines, and 10 EPS graphics to create custom documents for class, business, or even home use. Templates are supplied. Titles may be

curved or straight. MacPaint and EPS images may be imported to enhance productions. EPS images may be resized as needed. It supports all built-in and downloadable PostScript fonts up to 72 points. A special merge feature permits creation of certificates for an entire class or group of people.

Name:	**3-D Charts to Go!**
Program type:	Chart maker
Vendor:	BLOCPublishing Corp.
Cost:	$99.95
Hardware requirements:	IBM compatible; 640KB RAM minimum; 1.5MB disk space
Additional software needed:	Windows 3.0
Description:	The program draws magnificent charts of any type in 3-D. Files for charting can be imported from other programs, such as Lotus and Excel, and exported to PageMaker and similar desktop publishing programs. Charts may contain up to 2,250 data values. The system will import Meta File, PCX, and BMP graphics.
Review source:	*PC User*, February 12, 1992, 86.

Word Processing Programs with Graphics Capability

It is difficult to find a word processing program that only processes words these days. The top word processing programs all do some form of graphics and text integration. WordPerfect and Microsoft Word are the two leaders at the moment, but even WordStar, which has long been popular, has been overhauled to include graphics.

The advantage of these programs is that a person does not have to invest money or time in a separate system. The disadvantage is that the word processors are simply not as capable as the full-fledged systems discussed elsewhere in this book. If the major need is word processing, then a word processor with graphics editing capability may be the best choice. However, be prepared to find many tools missing, including little if any paint/draw support, etc. A major advantage of a program such as Print Shop over trying to do the same thing with Word-Perfect is the ease of use that Print Shop offers for creating page layouts.

Most medium-sized libraries will require the purchase of a major word processing system, a desktop publishing program, and perhaps even a number of auxiliary programs. A small library, however, may well make do with fewer programs.

Name:	**Ami Pro 3.0 for Windows**
Program type:	Word processor
Vendor:	Lotus Development Corp.
Cost:	$239
Hardware requirements:	IBM compatible
Additional software needed:	Windows 3.x
Description:	Ami Pro is an outstanding word processor with many features for use with the Windows environment. Context-sensitive help is provided throughout, an especially useful feature for novices. The Clean Screen option leaves the desktop completely uncluttered for work. There are many special features with word processing and desktop

publishing characteristics that rival WordPerfect. The program also includes a Quickstart tutorial.

Review source: *PC Computing*, December 1992, 156.

Name: **MacWrite**
Program type: Word processor
Vendor: Claris Corp.
Cost: $129
Hardware requirements: Macintosh
Description: MacWrite is an excellent word processing program with many desktop publishing features. It has font selection from 2 to 500 points, multiple columns, WYSIWYG display, footnotes, and headers; can crop and scale images (supports PICT or PICT2 graphics); and has context sensitive help files. The word processor also contains a spell check system. Commonly used combinations of fonts, styles, etc., can be easily stored in one file for later use.
Review source: *MacUser*, January 1991, 156.

Name: **Microsoft Word 5.0**
Program type: Word processor
Vendor: Microsoft Corp.
Cost: $495
Hardware requirements: Macintosh
Description: This is a top-of-the-line word processing program for the Macintosh and it has many desktop publishing capabilities. Word offers multicolumn text creation for newsletters. The system is easy to use. Simple style sheets can be generated for formatting material.
Review sources: *Byte*, February 1992, 47; *MacUser*, Annual, 1993, 309.

Name: **Microsoft Word for Windows 2.0**
Program type: Word processor
Vendor: Microsoft Corp.
Cost: $495
Hardware requirements: IBM compatible
Additional software needed: Windows 3.x
Description: This word processor offers many of the same features as Word for the Macintosh. The Windows format offers full integration with other IBM and Windows compatible programs.
Review source: *PC Computing*, December 1992, 156.

Name:	**WordPerfect 5.1**
Program type:	Word processor
Vendor:	WordPerfect Corp.
Cost:	$384
Hardware requirements:	IBM compatible; 384KB RAM minimum; 4MB disk space
Additional software available:	WordPerfect Presentations 2.0 and WordPerfect for Windows (a package that offers charts, drawing, and presentations), WordPerfect Screen Font Editor (a program for editing screen character appearance), WordPerfect Work (an integrated package that contains modules for word processing, graphics editing, drawing, communications, spreadsheet, and a desktop organizer), and WordPerfect Art, Vols. 1–5 (listed in clip art section, following).
Description:	WordPerfect is a word processing program that has many desktop publishing capabilities. It will manipulate tables, sort, produce outlines, make font changes, and permit the import of graphics. It has excellent control over spacing. Some of the outstanding characteristics included in the latest version of this program include indexing, automatic referencing, block protection, seven different column styles. Boxes can be created to hold graphics, sidebars, etc. Graphics files for WordPerfect are readily identified by the extension .WPG.
Additional source of information:	McClure, Rhyder, and Steven Cherry, *Desktop Publishing with WordPerfect 5.0 and 5.1*. New York: Simon & Schuster, 1990. This really excellent "how to" source for desktop publishing with WordPerfect gives command-by-command instructions for creating the common graphic procedures.

Name:	**WordPerfect 5.2 for Windows**
Program type:	Word Processor
Vendor:	WordPerfect Corp.
Cost:	$179
Hardware requirements:	IBM compatible; 4MB RAM minimum; 12MB disk space
Additional software needed:	Windows 3.x
Description:	This program is similar to WordPerfect 5.1, but it has many Windows additions, such as a mouse button bar, features specifically designed to aid with desktop publishing, and many more general features, thus making it a top choice for the highest levels of work. Many add-on

modules give it a wide range of utility, including clip art, other application packages, etc.

Review source: *PC User*, 18 November 1992, 18.

Name: **WordPerfect for Macintosh 2.1**
Program type: Word processor
Vendor: WordPerfect Corp.
Cost: $495
Hardware requirements: Macintosh; 1MB RAM minimum
Description: The program is much like the PC DOS version but for the Macintosh. It contains graphics and drawing capability, macro editor, multicolumn format, text wraparound, etc., and works with WPG, TIFF, EPS, PICT, PICT2, and GIF graphic formats in gray scale.

Name: **WordStar for Windows 1.5**
Program type: Word processor
Vendor: WordStar International Inc.
Cost: $495
Hardware requirements: IBM compatible
Description: WordStar was the first major word processing system available for microcomputers. It has been overtaken by others in recent years, but it is still available and has a loyal following. The new Windows version has many new and exciting features, including very capable use of text and graphics.

Painting and Drawing Programs

Although painting and drawing programs require additional skill to use, they provide great opportunity both in creating original art and in customizing clip art. They also make the whole job of creating much easier for anyone. For instance, a drawing program will create and size exact circles, squares, and other shapes with ease. With a mouse a user can use freehand brush strokes to create true works of art of all kinds or to revise an already existing graphic. There is usually some distinction between a painting and a drawing program. Most of the products in this section offer both functions. They also can be used to "paint" in various colors and to fill in patterns. Some offer an incredible number of options such as spray cans, line widths, stacking, and layering. Stacking objects can overlay each other on a page without actually removing them. This technique allows objects to be "hidden" until needed or moved. Layering is a technique that allows for greater ease of control over the many stacked objects that may accumulate. Separate layers may be created for graphic elements, text, etc.

Another type of program is for use by or with children. An example, Kid Pix, is listed in the school section of this book.

Name:	**Adobe Illustrator 4.0**
Program type:	Draw/paint
Vendor:	Adobe Systems, Inc.
Cost:	$595
Hardware requirements:	Macintosh, Apple IIGS, or IBM compatible; 2MB RAM minimum
Description:	This highly professional drawing program provides a multitude of tools. Users have access to automatic tracing of scanned objects to create instant line art that can be further edited and redrawn as required. Illustrator uses PostScript page description language to create images for processing. Thus, its products are said to be resolution-independent, or the result of an algorithm. Productions are saved as EPS format. Images can be assigned percent-

age of gray, primary process colors, or a Pantone Matching System color. Special zoom features will enlarge or reduce the image for viewing and editing. Shape tools include curve, ellipse, type, freehand, auto trace, pen, rectangle, oval, blend, scale, rotate, reflect, shear, scissors, measure, and page. Some missing features include no grids and no coordinates for placing work.

Review source: *MacWorld*, February 1991, 196.

Name: **Adobe Illustrator for Windows 4.0**
Program type: Draw/paint
Vendor: Adobe Systems, Inc.
Cost: $495
Hardware requirements: IBM compatible; 4MB RAM minimum; 1.44MB disk space
Additional software needed: Windows 3.x
Description: This highly professional Windows version of the drawing program in the preceding description provides a multitude of tools. Users have access to automatic tracing of scanned objects to create instant line art that can be further edited and redrawn as required. Illustrator uses PostScript page description language to create images for processing. Thus, its products are said to be resolution-independent, or the result of an algorithm. Productions are saved as EPS format. Images can be assigned percentage of gray, primary process colors, or a Pantone Matching System color. Special zoom features will enlarge or reduce the image for viewing and editing. Shape tools include curve, ellipse, type, freehand, auto trace, pen, rectangle, oval, blend, scale, rotate, reflect, shear, scissors, measure, and page. Some missing features include no grids and no coordinates for placing work.

Name: **CA-Cricket Draw III**
Program type: Draw/paint
Vendor: Computer Associates International, Inc.
Cost: $249
Hardware requirements: Macintosh; 2MB RAM minimum; 3MB disk space
Description: This version is a major improvement over the previous one. It includes many new features plus vastly expanded old ones. For instance, the color support has grown from 8 colors in the old Cricket Draw to 16 million. In addition, it supports gray-scale, HLS, RGB, CMYK, and

Pantone Matching System color models. Colors are available through a useful floating palette. Both Bezier curves and PostScript are supported. Other improvements include better text handling, a user-friendly interface, and the ability to import PICT, ESP, and MacPaint file formats. It will export in PICT or EPS formats. TIFF is not supported.

Review source: *MacWeek*, February 17, 1992, 51.

Name: **Canvas 3.0**
Program type: Draw/paint
Vendor: Deneba Systems
Cost: $399
Hardware requirements: Macintosh
Description: Canvas is a drawing program suitable mainly for technical and business applications. It also offers excellent text-handling capability, including kerning, spell checking, and many other word processing features, such as right justification, centering, etc., and will convert TrueType and PostScript fonts to curves.
Review source: *MacWorld*, January 1992, 163.

Name: **Cheap Paint**
Program type: Draw/paint
Vendor: Public Domain Exchange
Cost: $9 (shareware)
Hardware requirements: Apple IIgs
Description: This high-resolution paint program has basic drawing tools including pencil/paintbrush and airbrush with six spray patterns. It can draw lines, circles, rectangles, squares, arcs, curves, and polygons. The program also supports animation and special effects. Any area may be selected, cut, and then pasted elsewhere. Fine detailing is achieved by enlarging a segment and editing a pixel at a time. Two canvases can be used at one time and material moved between them.

Name: **CorelDraw! 3.0**
Program type: Draw/paint
Vendor: Corel Systems Corp.
Cost: $595
Hardware requirements: IBM compatible; 4MB RAM minimum; 32MB disk space

Additional software needed: Microsoft Windows

Additional software available: CorelShow

Description: This impressive program is more than just a draw-and-paint package. It also does charts and presentations. In fact, it is difficult to think of this new version as anything less than a page-layout program. Objects can be edited in layers, making it possible to directly edit text. Charts can be created in three-dimensional mode. Photos can be manipulated using an included version of ZSoft's Photo-Finish. Slides can be created using CorelShow for both on-screen presentations and for hard-copy slides. Product also comes with CD-ROM of 12,000 clip art images, 250 TrueType fonts, and templates.

Review sources: *PC World*, February 1992, 214; *PC Sources*, October 1992, 290.

Name: **Deluxe Paint II Enhanced 1.0**

Program type: Draw/paint

Vendor: Electronic Arts

Cost: $134.95

Hardware requirements: IBM compatible

Description: This program offers many unusual features, some of which are not to be found in other programs. For example, Deluxe Paint offers "multicolor sculpted" fonts and allows the user to adjust the contrast or brightness of any part of any image. Images may be printed out poster sized or converted to a slide for use in the Gallery slide show module. It supports PCX files and VGA/MCGA and EVGA graphics.

Additional features are many. Ten built-in brushes are provided. A toolbox contains the following tools: dotted freehand tool for fast drawing, continuous freehand tool, and straight-line, curve, fill, airbrush, rectangle, circle, ellipse, and polygon tools. Special effects include gradient and pattern fills, contrast and brightness adjustment, stencils, tinting effects such as shadows, magnifying and zooming, mirror, tile and point, cyclic symmetry, rotation, color cycling, colorizing, and smoothing.

Name: **Designer**

Program type: Draw/paint

Vendor: Micrografx

Cost: $484

Hardware requirements: IBM compatible; 1MB RAM minimum; 20MB disk storage

Additional software needed: Microsoft Windows 3.x

Description: Designer is a general-purpose graphics package intended to help in the creation of forms, maps, charts, graphics, technical drawings, diagrams, posters, illustrations, and many other tasks. It relies on Microsoft Windows for the user interface.

Designer creates object-oriented graphics on a grid canvas. The techniques of layering and stacking provide unusual power to this program. From the main menu users may access file, edit, draw, view, change (object editing), arrange (object manipulation), line style, pattern fill, text effects, and help.

Name: **DeskPaint and DeskDraw**

Program type: Draw/paint

Vendor: Zedcor, Inc.

Cost: $199.95

Hardware requirements: Macintosh; 99KB RAM

Description: These two programs that are bundled together provide a large variety of tools and capabilities as they interface with each other. Together the programs require only 99KB of memory. They can be used to create or edit many illustrations and graphics for newsletters, flyers, etc., including scanned images. DeskPaint supports TIFF, PICT, and MacPaint files. DeskDraw includes an object-oriented editor and a number of special effects. DeskDraw supports PICT images. The system has good speed and will handle colors and PostScript and other printers.

Review source: *MacWorld*, January 1992, 133; *Byte*, June 1991, 264.

Name: **Desktop Paint**

Program type: Draw/paint

Vendor: Software Labs

Cost: $3.69 (shareware)

Hardware requirements: IBM graphics, Microsoft-compatible mouse, hard disk drive: Epson-compatible printer, HP LaserJet-compatible, or PostScript printer

Additional software needed: Desktop layout program

Description: Desktop Paint is a bit-mapped paint program to edit images for use with desktop layout programs such as

PageMaker and Publish It! It comes with many useful editing tools: copy, cut/paste, invert, fill, font size, airbrush, etc. Files supported include MacPaint and PFS .MAC, Ventura, PC-Paintbrush, and WordPerfect. It does *not* support: CorelDraw! or Designer files.

Name:	**Desktop Painter**
Program type:	Draw/paint
Vendor:	Public Domain Exchange
Cost:	$9 (shareware)
Hardware requirements:	Apple IIGS
Description:	An inexpensive paint program, Desktop Painter contains numerous tools such as an airbrush, a pencil for freehand drawing, a paint can for solid colors, a font tool for working with installed fonts, a Bezier curve tool for creating smooth curves and radii, two square tools (sharp and rounded corners), a circle/oval tool, and two polygon tools. It supports sixteen colors for lines or solids. Editing supports cut and paste, copy, undo, and clear. The Invert command will produce a negative of the screen. Horizonal Flip produces a mirror image of an object and Vertical Flip produces an upside-down image. The program is accessible as a desk accessory.

Name:	**816/Paint**
Program type:	Draw/paint
Vendor:	Baudville Computer Products
Cost:	$75
Hardware requirements:	Apple II family
Additional software available:	Check with Apple about other programs in this series: 816/Animation, 816/Publish, and 816/Draw.
Description:	This is the only paint program for the Apple II series that is complete. Four separate modules work for each graphics mode. Additional utilities will work with DOS 3.3 and ProDOS disks. Tools include rotate, scale, stretch, and paint. The program uses Macintosh-like menus and supports Apple IIc and IIe Standard, Double, and Super Hi-Res graphics. Super Hi-Res mode supports a 4,096-color palette. The 816 refers to the program's support for both 8- and 16-bit Apple IIs.

Name:	**Expert Color Paint**
Program type:	Draw/paint
Vendor:	Softsync

Cost:	$49.95
Hardware requirements:	Macintosh
Description:	This inexpensive coloring program is an excellent place for beginners to try out many excellent paint features. The program includes fifteen levels of undo for chronic mind-changers. Its virtual memory feature will act as though the machine has much more RAM available than it really does. It supports only MacPaint, PICT, and TIFF formats.
Review source:	*MacWorld*, June 1992, 210.

Name:	**Fontasy**
Program type:	Draw/paint
Vendor:	Brown-Wagh Publishing
Cost:	$129.95
Hardware requirements:	IBM compatible
Description:	Fontasy, a low-end package, offers page layout of text and graphics. Libraries can make newsletters, flyers, signs, posters, and much more. It includes clip art, zoom feature, popup menus, and extensive help files.

Name:	**Freehand 3.1**
Program type:	Draw/paint
Vendor:	Aldus Corp.
Cost:	$595
Hardware requirements:	Macintosh
Description:	The newest version of Freehand is a drawing program that will satisfy even the most-advanced or serious graphics users. Its most noteworthy feature is the pressure-sensitive freehand tool that allows variable line weight. The system also supports PICT format, TrueType fonts, and Bezier curves.
Review sources:	*MacWorld*, June 1992, 202; *PC Magazine*, November 10, 1992, 275.

Name:	**Freehand 3.0 for Windows**
Program type:	Draw/paint
Vendor:	Aldus Corp.
Cost:	$595
Hardware requirements:	IBM compatible
Description:	Freehand has many features. It is, however, a program for advanced users with advanced needs. Most librarians will not need a drawing program of this sophistication.
Review sources:	*PC Computing*, April 1992, 40; *PC Sources*, January 1992, 72.

Name:	**Graphics Department**
Program type:	Draw/paint
Vendor:	Sensible Software
Cost:	$124.95
Hardware requirements:	Apple II series; supports Applemouse.
Description:	An adaptable color program in Graphics Department creates graphics for home and school use. It is good for business charts, lettering, graphic manipulation, charts (bar, area, line, 2-dimensional, 3-dimensional, scatter, and X-Y). Forty fonts in five sizes and six colors and six orientations are included. Tools will draw ellipses, points, lines, and rectangles. The Slide Projector module displays a slide show on monitor.

Name:	**MacPaint 2.0**
Program type:	Draw/paint
Vendor:	Claris Corp.
Cost:	$124.95
Hardware requirements:	Macintosh; 512KB RAM minimum; 500KB disk storage
Description:	An excellent program for creating artwork for various applications, MacPaint includes many good tools, including editing with undo, cut, paste, clear, invert, fill, trace edges, flip horizontally and vertically, and rotate. A special ''Goodies'' menu will turn the placement grid on or off, zoom in or out of a picture, list shortcuts, and allow for various preference settings. The font menu will list all fonts that have been installed with the Font/DA Mover program to the Macintosh system. More than three dozen patterns for shading a document are provided. A good variety of tools lets users change line weight and create rectangles, ovals, freehand shapes, and polygons. A grabber tool will scroll within the document in various directions. Others include a paint bucket, spray can, paintbrush, pencil, text tool, and eraser. One exciting aspect of MacPaint is the documentation, which is not clouded with excess explanations. It is short and concise, and it is easy to find what you need.

Name:	**Paint n' Print**
Program type:	Draw/paint
Vendor:	Expert Software
Cost:	$14.95
Hardware requirements:	IBM compatible

Description: This extremely inexpensive paint program can be used for versatile projects: ads, cards, announcements, and presentations.

Name: **PC Paint 3.1**
Program type: Draw/paint
Vendor: Mouse Systems Corp.
Cost: $69.95
Hardware requirements: IBM compatible
Description: A professional-quality package for creating original art, PC Paint offers a wide range of graphics tools that make creation of art relatively painless even for nonartists and beginners. Included are 80 different paint brushes, 60 predefined patterns, and 36 fills. The system also produces lines, arcs, open and closed curves, boxes, circles, ovals, and polygons, plus special effects such as flip, rotate, invert, stretch, and compress. Users have access to 256 simultaneous screen colors from a palette total of 262,144 colors. PC Paint is an excellent choice for anyone who has limited time or artistic talent but who wants a chance to create high quality materials. It works with dot matrix, color, ink jet, laser jet, and PostScript laser printers. GIF, PCX, PIC, IMG, and BSAVE formats are supported.

Name: **PC Paintbrush**
Program type: Draw/paint
Vendor: ZSoft Corp.
Cost: $99.95
Hardware requirements: IBM compatible
Description: PC Paintbrush is a full draw and paint program that uses the PCX format. Its features include 256 colors, screen capture, 3-D shadowed letters, etc. Overall, it is a versatile program that provides for creating, editing, and enhancing images.

Name: **PixelPaint Professional 2.0**
Program type: Draw/paint
Vendor: SuperMac Software
Cost: $799
Hardware requirements: Macintosh
Description: This is a high-level tool for professional design work. It includes image compositing, masking, transparency, and

even special effects such as embossing, tinting, controlled-image warping, etc. PixelPaint uses pressure-sensitive tools and virtual memory to scroll through larger documents that otherwise would not fit into RAM.

Review source: *MacWorld*, September 1991, 209.

Name: **SuperPaint 3.0**

Program type: Draw/paint

Vendor: Silicon Beach Software, Inc.

Cost: $199

Hardware requirements: Macintosh

Description: The SuperPaint program provides a painting and drawing environment for people with moderate needs. Most librarians would find it sophisticated enough to create many documents for public use. It includes texture fills and image-enhancement capabilities and can import EPS textures from other programs. Good color support is now available in this program, including 16- and 24-bit color. Artwork can be edited and saved in color. This should be considered a low-end paint tool that lacks many features of other versions listed. However, it is an excellent package for general graphics work.

Review source: *MacWorld*, March 1992, 179; *Computer Shopper*, February 1992, 630; *MacUser*, April 1992, 52.

Presentation Software Packages

Presentations come in various forms. All of the software in this section, however, creates some type of presentation material, including charts, slides, graphs, overhead transparencies, and even animation. Packages listed in this section differ widely as to their capability and their specific applications. A few make only slides: others have paint/draw capability. Harvard Graphics is an exceptional program for creating business charts.

Name:	**Business Graphics**
Program type:	Presentation graphics
Vendor:	Melody Hall
Cost:	$9.95
Hardware requirements:	IBM compatible
Description:	The package will take numerical data and convert them to graphs and charts. It is a memory-resident program.

Name:	**CA-Cricket Presents**
Program type:	Presentation graphics
Vendor:	Computer Associates
Cost:	$199
Hardware requirements:	Macintosh; 2MB RAM minimum; 3 to 5MB disk space
Description:	A medium-range presentation package, CA-Cricket Presents can import and customize templates to create slides. The program has a built-in spreadsheet for making work with charts simple. Its drawbacks include an inability to edit background material or to use existing text in a new template.
Review source:	*MacWorld*, July 1992, 156.

Name:	**CA-Cricket Presents for Windows**
Program type:	Presentation graphics
Vendor:	Computer Associates
Cost:	$199
Hardware requirements:	IBM compatible; 2MB RAM minimum; 3 to 5MB disk space
Additional software needed:	Windows 3.x
Description:	A medium-range presentation package, CA-Cricket Presents can import and customize templates to create slides. The program has a built-in spreadsheet for making work with charts simple. Its drawbacks include an inability to edit background material or to use existing text in a new template.

Name:	**Freelance 2.0**
Program type:	Presentation graphics
Vendor:	Lotus Development Corp.
Cost:	$495
Hardware requirements:	IBM compatible
Description:	Freelance is an easy-to-use package for creating presentation graphics. It comes with useful templates, ''SmartMasters,'' for aiding in the design process. Advanced features include sound and animation. It also contains an organizational-chart module.
Review sources:	*Byte*, February 1992, 48; *PC Computing*, December 1992, 48.

Name:	**Freelance Graphics for Windows 2.0**
Program type:	Presentation graphics
Vendor:	Lotus Development Corp.
Cost:	$495 ($150 upgrade)
Hardware requirements:	IBM compatible
Additional software needed:	Windows 3.x
Description:	Freelance is an easy-to-use package for creating presentation graphics. It comes with useful templates, ''SmartMasters,'' for aiding in the design process. Advanced features include sound and animation. It also contains an organizational-chart module.
Review source:	*PC Magazine*, November 10, 1992, 275.

Name:	**Harvard Graphics 3.05**
Program type:	Business charting
Vendor:	Software Publishing Corp.
Cost:	$595
Hardware requirements:	IBM compatible; 438KB RAM minimum; 4.5–12.2MB disk storage
Description:	Harvard Graphics is a highly advanced charting program. It is probably the best program of its kind available, ideal for anyone needing high-quality, specialized charts. It is especially designed for creating text, pie, bar, line, area, high/low/close, and organization charts. The built-in text charts allow for several types of lists to be displayed for slides, overhead transparencies, or other presentations.

Other charts are available in great variety. The pie chart, for example, can be exploded (sections being emphasized by being pulled out of the whole pie). The various types of charts can be used together, such as using a pie chart with a bar chart to provide analysis of a segment of a pie chart. Elements can be made 3-D as well.

Charts can also be specified by a color selection chart and have a variety of bold, italic, size, and underline fonts.

Graphics are easily included from the symbol library. The wide variety of graphics includes computers, animals, buildings, outlines, arrows, money, stars, humans, etc.

Review source:	*PC Computing*, January 1992, 42.

Name:	**Harvard Graphics 1.0 for Windows**
Program type:	Presentation graphics
Vendor:	Software Publishing Corp.
Cost:	$595
Hardware requirements:	IBM compatible; 4MB RAM minimum; 14MB disk space
Additional software needed:	Windows 3.x
Description:	This newer version of Harvard Graphics is much easier to use than the older one, described previously.
Review sources:	*InfoWorld*, June 22, 1992, 108; *PC Magazine*, February 25, 1992, 37.

Name: **Hollywood 1.1**
Program type: Presentation graphics
Vendor: Claris Corp.
Cost: $499
Hardware requirements: IBM compatible; 1.6MB RAM minimum; 2MB disk space
Additional software needed: Windows 3.x
Description: Hollywood was created originally by IBM and then sold to Claris (a subsidiary of Apple Computer, Inc.). This presentation package has a large number of features, including outliner. Work usually starts in outliner to organize presentation ideas. Switching back and forth to the presentation module is easy. The two are integrated, so that a change in the outliner makes corresponding changes in the presentation. Templates make work look more professional with less effort. Users create an outline and then choose a template. The presentation is formatted automatically and can be previewed on screen. Paint and draw tools are part of the package; scalable fonts are included as well.
Review sources: *PC World*, February 1992, 213; *Publish*, February 1992, 76.

Name: **Persuasion 2.12**
Program type: Presentation graphics
Vendor: Aldus Corp.
Cost: $495
Hardware requirements: Macintosh; 2MB RAM minimum; 20MB disk space
Description: Material can be organized with an outliner or word processor and then made into high-quality slides or overhead presentations. Persuasion comes with many predefined templates for quick creation of slides. Users can also create their own templates. Templates may be combined, previewed, and changed. The program will produce many charts and graphs and has fifteen wipe-and-dissolve special effects. Slides can be manually changed or automatically viewed. An idea outliner, word processor, spell checker, graphics editor, and chart module are included.

Name:	**Persuasion for Windows 3.0**
Program type:	Presentation graphics
Vendor:	Aldus Corp.
Cost:	$495
Hardware requirements:	IBM compatible; 2MB RAM minimum; 20 to 40MB disk space
Additional software needed:	Windows 3.x
Description:	This package comes with many predefined templates for quick creation of slides, or new templates can be easily created from scratch. Templates may be combined, previewed, and changed. The program will produce many charts and graphs and has fifteen wipe-and-dissolve special effects. Slides can be manually changed or put into fully automatic demo mode. AutoTemplate, a program for using predefined page layouts from spreadsheets and word processors, is included. The program will exchange files from IBM compatibles and Macintoshes. The idea outliner is included.

Integrated Software

Integrated software is an important class of products. For some years integration has been the trend, but this has been less necessary with the advent of Windows and GUIs. Nevertheless, an integrated software package, such as Microsoft Works, gives the user access to a range of products integrated as modules. Data can be swapped between modules, often automatically. For example, material in a spreadsheet can be turned into charts with little additional effort. The best of such software offers word processing, spreadsheets, graphics, telecommunications, and database management all in one. The shortcoming of such packages is that the user is stuck with all of the modules, the quality of which may be uneven. If a user has little need of database management, for example, but high-level need for desktop publishing, then integrated software is not the exclusive answer.

Name:	**BeagleWorks 1.01**
Program type:	Integrated software
Vendor:	Beagle Brothers Micro Software, Inc.
Cost:	$299.95
Hardware requirements:	Macintosh; 1MB RAM minimum
Description:	BeagleWorks, a fully integrated package, offers word processor, spreadsheet, charting, database manager, draw, paint, and communications. The word processor will wrap text around imported objects, format in multiple columns, create multiple headers and footers, and use Microlytics spelling checker and thesaurus. It is excellent for creating newsletters and other simple documents. The chart component will create good line, bar, column, area, scatter, exploded pie, or other charts using 256 custom colors.

The paint component includes paintbrush, spray can, paint bucket, pencil, line, arc, freehand shape, special effects, and others. The module draw contains many drawing tools for lines, rectangles, polygons, etc. Both modules contain 128 patterns and 256 colors.

The spreadsheet component will handle a sizable 256 columns and 16,385 rows. The database module manages 256 fields per record and has 64 built-in functions. In addition, thirty-two report formats are ready for use.

Review sources: *inCider/A +*, February 1992, 28; *Computer Shopper*, November 1992, 684.

Name: **ClarisWorks**
Program type: Integrated software
Vendor: Claris Corp.
Cost: $299
Hardware requirements: Macintosh
Description: This program is a fully integrated system capable of word processing, spreadsheet applications, database management, telecommunications, and graphics. The graphics module includes page layout of text, clip art, and charts. The program directly produces a WYSIWYG screen of the document without preview or thumbnail sketch necessary. Drawing tools are easy to use and include pen widths, pattern fill, etc. Text can be rotated sideways or upside down. Extensive help files are included. This sophisticated program will do many complicated jobs for librarians. The word processing module contains a dictionary of 100,000 words.

Name: **Lotus 1-2-3**
Program type: Integrated software
Vendor: Lotus Development Corp.
Cost: $595
Hardware requirements: IBM compatibles
Description: The main function of this program is the spreadsheet; subsidiary to it are the database manager and the graphics. Although it was the first impressive integrated software package, this program has no word processor. Lotus 1-2-3 has been extremely popular as a high-level business system. The new version contains many improvements, including the ability to install it on a local area network.

Most popular in the system is the spreadsheet; all other components are subordinate to it and unable to function without it. For example, the information manager component (not database manager), with essentially the same grid as the spreadsheet component, uses data from the spreadsheet; the graphics system captures and also uses data from the spreadsheet.

The system comes with a six-lesson tutorial that covers all major functions, making start-up uncomplicated even for novices. Computation and recalculations of this assembly-language program are fast, and there is extensive online help. Lotus 1-2-3 has five basic charts: bar, stacked bar, side-by-side bar, pie, and scatter. They are created with simple keystrokes, a great advantage over earlier and less-sophisticated spreadsheets such as Visi-Calc. Essentially, all operation modes may be carried out with the same command structure.

Name:	**Microsoft Works for Windows**
Program type:	Integrated software
Vendor:	Microsoft Corp.
Cost:	$199
Hardware requirements:	IBM compatibles; 5MB disk space
Additional software needed:	Windows 3.x
Description:	The program encompasses word processing, spreadsheets, charts, database management and reports, and communications. It is also fairly easy to use. Most of the components are sophisticated and interactive enough to provide a real work environment. The program also has many desktop publishing features. The system will easily import PCX, TIFF, and BMP images into the drawing module. Six chart styles will create good-looking charts. The program's database management system is a version of Excel that holds 32,000 records for retrieval in a variety of ways.
Review source:	*PC World*, November 1991, 128.

Utility Programs

At one time or another, anyone using a microcomputer will suddenly find that there is something that they need to do that neither their everyday programs nor the utilities built into the Macintosh and DOS and Windows will do. There are hundreds of auxiliary programs available to meet such needs. These fall into several categories.

Since the computer world has few real standards, many data formats are incompatible. Special utilities will convert graphics as well as text from one format to another. This is especially important when working with clip art or when a finished product must be moved from one package to another.

Other utility packages range from screen savers (programs that protect a monitor screen from "burn-in" when it is not in use) to memory management packages (programs that reallocate memory resources in a computer for maximum efficiency). Screen capture programs will convert computer screen images for use in word processed documents as clip art. Programs such as Grammatik are also listed. These help a writer improve the content of documents by checking spelling, grammar, and style. Those programs that are specifically relevant to graphics are discussed in this section.

Printer programs will print spreadsheets and other products sideways (landscape) to make better use of paper and to reduce or eliminate the amount of cut and paste necessary. Other printer programs will improve the look of the printed page by producing "near laser quality" on a nonlaser printer.

Several other important utilities are also listed, including the Norton series. These cover virus protection, backup, and data recovery.

Name:	**Art Converter**
Program type:	Conversion program
Vendor:	Spinnaker Software Corp.
Cost:	$29.95
Hardware requirements:	Apple II series
Description:	Art Converter converts clip art files between formats. It supports Print Shop, Newsroom, Springboard Publisher, Works of Art, MousePaint, PrintMaster, Beagle Graph-

ics, Blazing Paddles, Dazzle Draw, as well as Hi-Res ProDOS and Hi-Res DOS 3.3.

Name:	**Capture**
Program type:	Screen capture
Vendor:	Mainstay
Cost:	$79.95
Hardware requirements:	Macintosh
Description:	This screen capture program permits the easy transfer of a Mac screen into a Word document.

Name:	**DoDOT 4.0**
Program type:	Image-file conversion desk accessory
Vendor:	Halcyon Software
Cost:	$189
Hardware requirements:	IBM compatible; 1.5MB RAM minimum; 4MB disk space
Additional software needed:	Windows 3.x
Description:	This system performs screen capture and image file format conversion in the Windows operating environment. Material is captured and put into Clipboard or sent to a printer or disk file all without leaving Windows. It supports twenty file formats, including TIFF, PCX, EPS (color and gray scale), GIF, BMP, WPG, MAC. Other features include color separation (red, green, blue, and black), image panning, zooming, resizing, and onscreen viewing of more than one page. The system prints preview pages and supports PostScript, PaintJet, LaserJet, and any Windows supported peripherals.
Review source:	*PC Magazine*, August 1991, 383.

Name:	**Effects Specialist**
Program type:	Font utility
Vendor:	Postcraft International, Inc.
Cost:	$180
Hardware requirements:	Macintosh; 1MB RAM minimum; 1MB disk space
Description:	The program makes available 120 special effects with bit-mapped or PostScript fonts. These include kerning, scaling, etc. Produces exportable EPS, PICT, or Clipboard files.

Name:	**Effects Specialist for Windows**
Program type:	Font utility
Vendor:	Postcraft International, Inc.

Cost:	$180
Hardware requirements:	IBM compatible; 1MB RAM minimum; 500KB disk space
Additional software needed:	Windows 3.x
Description:	The program makes available 120 special effects, with bit-mapped or PostScript fonts. These include kerning, scaling, etc. It produces exportable EPS, PICT, or Clipboard files.

Name:	**Freedom of Press Standard; Freedom of Press Light; Freedom of Press Pro**
Program type:	PostScript conversion utility
Vendor:	ColorAge, Inc.
Cost:	$255 (Freedom of Press Standard); $84 (Freedom of Press Light); $495 (Freedom of Press Pro)
Hardware requirements:	Macintosh; 2MB RAM (Standard), 640KB RAM (Light), 4MB RAM (Pro); IBM compatible
Description:	These three versions of the same program take PostScript files and print them on 50 different non-PostScript printers, including inkjet, dot matrix, and lasers. Adobe Type Manager and Adobe type fonts are supported. There are 35 scalable and rotatable outline fonts included. Freedom Light contains 17 fonts and supports 40 printers. Freedom Pro includes support for 24-bit color printers, additional high-end devices.

Name:	**Gallery Effects**
Program type:	Special effects library
Vendor:	Aldus Corp.
Cost:	$99
Hardware requirements:	Macintosh
Description:	The program enhances scanned and bit-mapped images in a variety of ways. Master effects included with variations include Charcoal, Chalk & Charcoal, Chrome, Craquelere, Dark Strokes, Poster Edges, Ripple, Smudge Stick, Spatter, Watercolor, Dry Brush, Emboss, Film Grain, and Fresco. All effects can be used as stand-alone format, as a desk accessory, as plug-in filters, with many standard applications, and with animator for PICS animations.

Name:	**Grammatik V**
Program type:	Writing improvement
Vendor:	Reference Software International

Cost:	$99
Hardware requirements:	IBM compatible; Macintosh; 640KB RAM minimum; 1.6MB disk space
Description:	Grammatik provides many checking features including spelling, usage, grammar, etc. Suggestions are made and final decisions regarding any changes are left to the user. However, the program does not find everything that is incorrect.

Name:	**Grammatik V for Windows 2.0**
Program type:	Writing improvement
Vendor:	Reference Software International
Cost:	$99
Hardware requirements:	IBM compatible; 2MB RAM minimum; 2.2MB disk space
Additional software needed:	Windows 3.x
Description:	The program comes included with WordPerfect 5.2 for Windows. It provides many checking features including spelling, usage, grammar, etc. Suggestions are made and final decisions regarding changes are left to the user. However, the program does not find everything that is incorrect.

Name:	**Graphics Link Plus for Windows**
Program type:	File conversion
Vendor:	TerraVision, Inc.
Cost:	$149
Hardware requirements:	IBM compatible; 384KB RAM minimum
Additional software needed:	Windows 3.x
Description:	This program converts graphic files to and from most major formats. Additional features include dithering/ trace, scaling, rotation, reverse, and conversion of color to gray scale.

Name:	**Image Alchemy 1.5**
Program type:	Image file conversion and compression
Vendor:	Handmade Software, Inc.
Cost:	$79.95
Hardware requirements:	IBM compatible; 400KB RAM minimum; 1MB disk space
Description:	The utility compresses PCX, GIF, TIFF, compressed TIFF, Deluxe Paint, TARGA, Sun Raster, RAW, and Macintosh files into a much smaller space using a special graphic compression technique (JPEG) so that files take

up much less space on disk. Files can also be browsed in compressed form with this program.

Name:	**MacLinkPlus/PC**
Program type:	File conversion program (PC to Mac)
Vendor:	DataViz Inc.
Cost:	$199; $699 (MacLinkPlus/Translators)
Hardware requirements:	Macintosh; IBM compatible
Description:	The program easily converts PC format word processing files from WordPerfect, Word for Windows, and Multimate into files for the Macintosh for use with Word. It also will convert in reverse order. The kit contains everything required for modem or cable transfer. A DOS Mounter to access 3.5-inch DOS disks also is included. Its impressive list of file conversion possibilities includes more than 400 combinations of file translators. DOS Mounter software allows for exchange of disks between Macs and PCs. A special icon, "drag-to-translate," makes conversion possible by just dragging the file over the MacLinkPlus icon. The system also keeps formatting of text, such as boldface, margins, tabs, underlines, etc., in place, and spreadsheet or database files can also be translated without loss of file format. Graphics files can be converted between computers and between applications "in any size." It works with Windows and networks. If your Mac and PC are already linked and able to exchange files, you may still wish to purchase the translators that are sold separately.

Name:	**Norton AntiVirus 2.1**
Program type:	Security
Vendor:	Symantec Corp.
Cost:	$129
Hardware requirements:	IBM compatible; 384KB RAM minimum
Additional software needed:	Windows 3.x
Description:	This program is highly recommended for dealing with computer viruses. Once installed, any or all disk drives may be scanned for 1,500 known viruses. In most cases, disks may be inoculated against the offending strains. It also checks RAM, has password protection, and has an ongoing protection feature that will scan all programs as they are loaded into the computer.

Name: **Norton Backup 2.0**
Program type: Backup utility
Vendor: Symantec Corp.
Cost: $129
Hardware requirements: IBM compatible; 512KB RAM minimum; 1.2MB disk space
Description: This program is insurance against hard disk drive failure. Data is stored on tape, then restored to the drive when needed. Data verification and compression are available in three levels.

Name: **Norton Backup for Windows 2.0**
Program type: Backup utility
Vendor: Symantec Corp.
Cost: $149
Hardware requirements: IBM compatible; 2MB RAM minimum
Additional software needed: Windows 3.x
Description: The program adds Windows features to basic backup functions. It backs up files in background when other applications are running. It will also run scheduled backups unattended.

Name: **Norton Disk Doctor**
Program type: Disk diagnostics
Vendor: Symantec Corp.
Cost: $149.95
Hardware requirements: IBM compatible
Description: The Norton Disk Doctor offers basic diagnostic utilities for remedying problems with boot record, file allocation table, and active storage areas. Additional features include checking disk sectors, making disks bootable, reviving disks, and more.

Name: **On-Side**
Program type: Printer utility
Vendor: Expressware Corp.
Cost: $24.95
Hardware requirements: IBM compatible; IBM or Epson compatible printer; 256KB minimum RAM
Additional software needed: Any program that can create an ASCII text file
Description: The program prints out any ASCII document landscape style (sideways). It is especially useful for spreadsheets. On-Side comes with seven different fonts (with font edi-

tor) that can be enlarged either vertically or horizontally; it also will create new or edit existing fonts.

Name:	**Picture Packer 3.0 and Picture Packer for Windows 2.0**
Program type:	Image file compression utility
Vendor:	Video & Image Compression Corp.
Cost:	$99 (each); $495 if bundled with accelerator card
Hardware requirements:	IBM compatible; Macintosh compatible (Picture Packer Accelerator Card optional)
Additional software needed:	Windows 3.x (Picture Packer for Windows)
Description:	This on-the-fly compressor/decompressor program (software and/or hardware) speeds compression and decompression of image files. It works with TIFF, PCX, GIF, and TARGA. The program has a memory-resident component that activates automatically and transparently with the current application. The Windows version takes advantage of that special operating system's features.
Review source:	*PC World*, August 1991, 110.

Name:	**PICTure This 2.0**
Program type:	Graphic format conversion utility
Vendor:	FGM, Inc.
Cost:	$149
Hardware requirements:	Macintosh; 1MB RAM minimum
Description:	The program converts twenty-four different graphics file formats to Macintosh PICT and PICT2 formats for use with Macintosh applications.

Name:	**PrintRite**
Program type:	Printer utility (spooler)
Vendor:	BLOCPublishing Corp.
Cost:	$30
Hardware requirements:	IBM compatible; 50KB RAM minimum
Description:	PrintRite lets a PC print without giving up control to the printer. Files are compressed and stored to disk. PrintRite will control up to five printers at one time, each doing different jobs, sideways, graphics, forms, or text. It will handle 255 documents and more than 65,000 copies at one time.

Name:	**Recognize! 2.0**
Program type:	Optical character recognition
Vendor:	NewDEST Corp.

Cost:	$695
Hardware requirements:	IBM compatible; Macintosh; 640KB RAM minimum; 4MB disk space
Description:	The program has Omnifont, an optical character recognition feature that makes it useful for translating more than 350 different fonts into ASCII text. It will also turn text directly into formats suitable for many popular word processors. It retains format codes for word processor documents, but it removes pictures from text.
Review source:	*Computer Shopper*, December 1990, 410.

Name:	**RightWriter 6.0**
Program type:	Writing improvement
Vendor:	Que Software
Cost:	$99
Hardware requirements:	IBM compatible; Macintosh; 1MB RAM minimum; 450KB disk space
Description:	This is an excellent tool for improving writing. The system covers grammar, punctuation, spelling, and even usage. Some 6,500 rules of good writing are covered. The program digests a completed manuscript and embeds its comments and suggestions as text within the document. The user then goes through the document with a word processor to make changes and improvements.

Name:	**RightWriter for Windows 6.0**
Program type:	Writing improvement
Vendor:	Que Software
Cost:	$99
Hardware requirements:	IBM compatible; 1MB RAM minimum; 1MB disk space
Additional software needed:	Windows 3.x
Description:	This is an excellent tool for improving writing. The system covers grammar, punctuation, spelling, and even usage. Some 6,500 rules of good writing are covered. The program digests a completed manuscript and embeds its comments and suggestions as text within the document. The user then goes through the document with a word processor to make changes and improvements.

Name:	**Sideways 3.3**
Program type:	Spreadsheet printer utility
Vendor:	Funk Software, Inc.
Cost:	$89.95

Hardware requirements:	IBM compatible; 80KB RAM minimum; 110KB disk space
Description:	Spreadsheets are often too large to fit horizontally onto a printed page. Instead of cutting and pasting, this program will do the work for you by turning the print sideways. Sideways has numerous options including margin adjustment, underlined and bold print, page size, borders, and nine typestyles.

Name:	**SmartScrap & The Clipper 2.1**
Program type:	Graphics manager
Vendor:	Portfolio Systems, Inc.
Cost:	$89.95
Hardware requirements:	Macintosh; 1MB RAM minimum; 100KB disk space
Description:	These two programs offer ease of use and storage of clip art. SmartScrap is a scrapbook program that organizes multiple scrapbooks of graphics. The program also has a pictorial table of contents with thumbnail miniatures of each item. The Clipper is used to manipulate a graphic copied to the clipboard. Tools include crop, shrink, and enlarge. It makes cutting, copying, and pasting much easier.

Name:	**TGL+ (The Graphics Link Plus) 2.0**
Program type:	File conversion
Vendor:	HSC Software
Cost:	$149
Hardware requirements:	IBM compatible; Macintosh; 384KB RAM minimum
Description:	TGL+ converts files to and from popular bitmap programs. It handles 17 formats including PCX, TIFF, WPG, and GIF. ESP, a nonbitmap format, is also supported. Additional utilities include screen-capture capabilities saved in PICTOR format. ASCII text files are easily captured and converted to PCX bitmap or any of eight fonts. A special Microsoft Windows capture utility is run from within Windows. The program also scales images up or down. Other features include color scale, auto-trace, and rotate images.

Typefaces and Fonts

To do any serious work, it is necessary to have a selection of fonts from which to choose. While many programs come with their own fonts, many add-on packages exist that can supply hundreds of additional fonts. These will provide an excellent variety for headlines and text.

Unfortunately, the terms used to describe type have not transitioned well from the printing industry to computers. They are used and defined in different ways in different publications. To understand type, it is necessary to understand several distinct terms.

Type is made up of characters. There is *body type* for the text in a document and *display type* for headlines. Type is measured in points, approximately 72 points to the inch. Display type used for headlines is usually 18 points and larger. Text type is usually 14 points and smaller. Another important concept is called *leading*. This refers to the space between the lines of type.

A complete set of the characters is a *character set*, which may include upper- and lowercase letters, numbers, punctuation marks, and dingbats. A *dingbat* is a special symbol such as degree signs, bullets, etc. A *font* is a complete set of characters in one typeface and size. An example is Courier New, 12 point. A *typeface*, on the other hand, is a particular style that also includes all sizes, for example, any size of Courier New. A *type family* includes related typefaces such as bold, italic, etc.

Font collections are now easy to find, though they can be costly. Once purchased, they must be installed on the computer system, usually on a hard disk drive. This can be a trick in itself, as can be keeping track of fonts. There are thousands of fonts in a variety of sizes and styles available for microcomputers. To change fonts on an electric typewriter, it is necessary to change the printwheel. A microcomputer program can make many more fonts available without changing a printwheel. Some classic fonts are Courier, Helvetica, and Times. Each of these may be used in bold, italic, or condensed forms.

Fonts also come as *serif* and *sans serif*. Serif fonts are distinctive because of the additional ornamentation (short crossing lines) on characters (serifs). Sans serif fonts, on the other hand, are plainer or cleaner. Serif fonts are often reserved for headline material. They look more stylish or graceful and are generally more readable than sans serif.

Similar to the process for making graphics larger or smaller, fonts may be created in several ways. *Bit-mapped* fonts are actual representations of the font in a dot pattern. Different scales of a font will require another set of the same font. The flaw of this system is that font variations will all take up more storage space on disk. The opposite of this is scalable fonts. They are represented by a mathematical formula that creates any size needed without taking up additional storage space. Scalable fonts are quickly winning first place in the computer world. They are more usable and are replacing bit-mapped fonts. TrueType (Upgrade Software) and PostScript (Adobe) are scalable fonts. They can be easily converted to any desirable size. This saves expense, computer disk space, and installation problems.

A collection of fonts needs to be manipulated in an organized fashion. Some special programs available for this are included in the list of products that follow.

Sources of Additional Information

Fenton, Erfert. *The Macintosh Font Book: Typographic Tips, Techniques and Resources.* Berkeley, Calif: Peachpit Press, 1989.

————. "Working with Fonts: A Hands-on Guide to Installation." *MacWorld* 8, no. 5:153 (May 1991).

Wil-Harris, Daniel. *Typestyle: How to Choose and Use Fonts on a Personal Computer.* Berkeley, Calif: Peachpit Press, 1990. The book includes techniques on the basic design selections needs of fonts. The material focuses on fonts available from Bitstream, Inc. 50 pages of illustrations.

Name:	**Adobe TypeAlign 1.0.4**
Program type:	Font utility
Vendor:	Adobe Systems, Inc.
Cost:	$99
Hardware requirements:	Macintosh; 1MB RAM minimum
Additional software needed:	Adobe Type Manager
Description:	This font utility allows for irregular placement of text anywhere on the page. Users can draw straight, curved, or any other type of line, and text will follow the same pattern. Also included is rotation, kerning, colorizing, manipulation, and distortion of text techniques.

Name:	**Adobe TypeAlign for Windows 2.1**
Program type:	Font utility
Vendor:	Adobe Systems, Inc.
Cost:	$99

Hardware requirements:	IBM compatible; 2MB RAM minimum; 500KB disk space
Additional software needed:	Windows 3.x; Adobe Type Manager
Description:	This font utility allows for irregular placement of text anywhere on the page. Users can draw straight, curved, or any other type of line, and text will follow the same pattern. Also included is rotation, kerning, colorizing, manipulation, and distortion of text techniques.

Name:	**Adobe Typeface Library**
Program type:	Font collection
Vendor:	Adobe Systems, Inc.
Cost:	$99
Hardware requirements:	IBM compatible; 512KB RAM minimum
Description:	The package contains 220 fonts and 1,000 typefaces. It supports IBM PostScript.

Name:	**Adobe Typeface Library for Windows**
Program type:	Font collection
Vendor:	Adobe Systems, Inc.
Cost:	$99
Hardware requirements:	IBM compatible; 512KB RAM minimum
Additional software needed:	Windows 3.x
Description:	The package contains 220 fonts and 1,000 typefaces with support for the IBM PostScript Interpreter.

Name:	**Adobe Type Manager 2.03**
Program type:	Font utility
Vendor:	Adobe Systems, Inc.
Cost:	$79.95 (Macintosh); $99 (IBM)
Hardware requirements:	Macintosh; IBM compatible; 1MB RAM minimum; 720KB disk space
Additional software available:	Adobe Type Manager Plus Pack, provides twenty-two additional type fonts and styles for use with this program for $198.
Description:	The Program will produce on-the-fly font enlargement or reduction of any PostScript outline font. It includes thirteen Adobe fonts.
Review source:	*PC Computing*, November 1990, 143.

Name:	**Adobe Type Manager for Windows 2.0**
Program type:	Type manager
Vendor:	Adobe Systems, Inc.

Cost:	$99
Hardware requirements:	IBM compatible; 1MB RAM minimum; 720KB disk space
Additional software needed:	Windows 3.x
Additional software available:	Adobe Type Manager Plus Pack, provides twenty-two additional type fonts and styles for use with this program for $198.
Description:	The Program will produce on-the-fly font enlargement or reduction of any PostScript outline font. It includes thirteen Adobe fonts.
Review source:	*PC Computing*, November 1990, 143.

Name:	**Adobe Type Reunion**
Program type:	Font manager
Vendor:	Adobe Systems, Inc.
Cost:	$65
Hardware requirements:	Macintosh
Description:	This program will automatically group fonts into families and styles, making their selection much easier. A submenu selects styles.

Name:	**Adobe Type Set I, II, and III**
Program type:	Font collections
Vendor:	Adobe Systems, Inc.
Cost:	$99 each (I and II); $198 (III)
Hardware requirements:	Macintosh; 640KB RAM minimum; 720KB disk space
Additional software needed:	Adobe Type Manager
Description:	Each package contains a dozen or so new add-on fonts for use with Adobe Type Manager.

Name:	**Adobe Type Set I, II, and III for Windows**
Program type:	Font collections
Vendor:	Adobe Systems, Inc.
Cost:	$99 each (I and II); $198 (III)
Hardware requirements:	IBM compatible; 1MB RAM minimum; 720KB disk space
Additional software needed:	Windows 3.x; Adobe Type Manager for Windows.
Description:	Each package contains a dozen or so new add-on fonts for use with the Adobe Type Manager for Windows.

Name:	**Adobe Type Set: Invitations & Awards**
Program type:	Font collection
Vendor:	Adobe Systems, Inc.

Cost:	$149
Hardware requirements:	Macintosh
Additional software needed:	Adobe Type Manager
Additional software available:	Letters, Memos & Faxes; Overheads & Slides; Spreadsheets & Graphs
Description:	This package provides additional fonts for use with the Adobe Type Manager: Arcadia, Fraktur, Snell Roundhand, Charlemagne, etc.

Name:	**Adobe Type Set: Invitations & Awards for Windows**
Program type:	Font collection
Vendor:	Adobe Systems, Inc.
Cost:	$149
Hardware requirements:	IBM compatible; 1MB RAM minimum; 720KB disk space
Additional software needed:	Adobe Type Manager for Windows
Additional software available:	Letters, Memos & Faxes for Windows; Overheads & Slides for Windows; Spreadsheets & Graphs for Windows
Description:	This package provides additional fonts for use with the Adobe Type Manager for Windows: Arcadia, Fraktur, Snell Roundhand, Charlemagne, etc.

Name:	**The Curator**
Program type:	Graphic file manager
Vendor:	Solutions International
Cost:	$139.95
Hardware requirements:	Macintosh
Additional software needed:	Microsoft Word (or other word processor or graphics program)
Description:	For users of large numbers of graphics, this system makes it easy to open and view files on a hard disk. The Curator will display all files with thumbnails, an entire folder at once. Graphics may be cut and pasted from most graphic file types. Files may also be converted from one file type to another. When used with Microsoft Word, the program will work with PICT, TIFF, and EPS files.

Name:	**Digi-Duit! and Digi-Fonts Basic Set**
Program type:	Font conversion
Vendor:	Digi-Fonts, Inc.
Cost:	$89.95
Hardware requirements:	IBM compatible; 512KB RAM minimum

Additional software needed: WordPerfect, Windows, Word, or Ventura Publisher, PageMaker

Additional software available: The Digi-Fonts Typeface Library ($399.95) offers 272 fonts that can be manipulated.

Description: Digi-Duit! is a font generator that creates LaserJet fonts from 3 to 720 points at 0.1-point increments. It takes a scalable font (eight included) and changes it to LaserJet-compatible soft fonts. Fonts come as blank outlines waiting to be manipulated in various ways; they can be expanded or condensed, slanted, flopped, rotated, reversed, or given portrait or landscape orientations. Fonts may be in outline form, shadowed, with various fill patterns, etc. The program offers mouse support, multiple symbol sets, and more. The system will automatically name and install or deinstall fonts.

Name: **Eye Relief**

Program type: Large-font word processor

Vendor: SkiSoft, Inc.

Cost: $295 (demo copy available)

Hardware requirements: IBM compatible

Description: For visually impaired persons this program can make reading the text on a computer screen much easier when doing word processing. Screen characters (including messages, menus, and document text) in six fonts range from 20 lines by 80 characters to 4 lines by 20 characters. This is a bare-bones system; features include word count, headers, footers, margin set. Users have wordwrap, find and replace, insert and overstrike, cut, copy, and paste, and even macros. Obvious by their absence are boldface, underlining, tabs, spelling checker. Some personal choices are allowable. For instance, the amount of white space between lines can be adjusted as can screen background and text colors (color changes require EGA or VGA graphics). Eye Relief will print on any ASCII or PostScript printer in normal-sized type. On an HP LaserJet or PostScript printer it can also print in 18 point. It comes with a 180-page manual that is in 18 point Times Roman.

Review source: *PC LapTop*, January 1991, 34.

Name: **Fluent Laser Font Library 4.0**

Program type: PostScript typefaces and styles

Vendor: Cassady & Greene, Inc.

Cost:	$99
Hardware requirements:	Macintosh
Additional software needed:	Software package that uses laser fonts
Description:	Collection of seventy-nine PostScript fonts and seventy-nine TrueType faces.

Name:	**Font Fixer**
Program type:	Font conversion
Vendor:	Public Domain Exchange
Cost:	$5 (shareware)
Hardware requirements:	Apple II
Additional software needed:	Publish It!
Description:	The program converts Apple IIGS fonts into fonts that can be used by the Publish It! desktop publishing program for the Apple II. Fifteen fonts are included. This is an excellent value for the price.

Name:	**FonTmax**
Program type:	Font utility
Vendor:	ISS International Software Systems, Inc.
Cost:	$129.95
Hardware requirements:	IBM compatible
Additional software needed:	WordPerfect
Description:	The program vastly expands the fonts available to WordPerfect, including Greek and Hebrew, Japanese, Russian, borders, chemistry, electronics, and many others. It comes with eighteen character sets, but others are available at $12 each. The system integrates into WordPerfect's menu system.

Name:	**The FontMonger 1.5**
Program type:	Type manipulation (conversion) program
Vendor:	Ares Software Corp.
Cost:	$149.95
Hardware requirements:	Macintosh; 2MB RAM minimum; 700KB disk space
Description:	FontMonger is an excellent go-between for most major font formats. It will convert characters or font sets into Adobe Illustrator, PostScript, and Windows metafile format. The program does an excellent job with a difficult task. It can be customized since it contains many options that can be changed according to the user's needs.
Review source:	*MacWorld*, October 1991, 162.

Name: **FontMonger for Windows 1.06**
Program type: Type manipulation (conversion) program
Vendor: Ares Software Corp.
Cost: $149.95
Hardware requirements: IBM compatible; 2MB RAM minimum; 1.5MB disk space
Additional software needed: Windows 3.x
Description: FontMonger is an excellent go-between for most major font formats. It will convert characters or font sets into Adobe Illustrator, PostScript, and Windows metafile format. The program does an excellent job with a difficult task. It can be customized since it contains many options that can be changed according to the user's needs.

Name: **Fonts and Borders 2.0**
Program type: Font collection
Vendor: Unison World Software
Cost: $34.95
Hardware requirements: IBM compatible
Additional software needed: PrintMaster or PrintMaster Plus
Description: This add-on package provides twenty new fonts ranging in size from 12 to 60 points. Also included are twenty new borders.

Name: **Glyphix 3.1**
Program type: Font collection
Vendor: SWFTE International, Ltd.
Cost: $99.95 per set
Hardware requirements: IBM compatible; 640KB RAM minimum
Additional software needed: WordPerfect
Description: Six different packages are available, each containing the following fonts: Basics, Basics II, Book, Sans Serif, Decorative, Fixed. It comes with automatic installation software for WordPerfect. The fonts are fully scalable from 3 to 120 points.

Name: **MenuFonts**
Program type: Font utility
Vendor: DUBL-Click
Cost: $59.95
Hardware requirements: Macintosh

Description: The program performs the useful function of displaying actual fonts in a menu prior to selecting a font by using the program's KeyScroll feature. Users may type the first letter of any font to select it. Its displays can be changed from 9 to 24 point.

Name: **Suitcase II**
Program type: Font manager
Vendor: Fifth Communication Systems, Inc.
Cost: $79; $89 with Pyro screensaver
Hardware requirements: Macintosh; 512KB RAM minimum; 40KB disk space
Description: The system provides easy and unlimited access to fonts, desk accessories, and function keys. Samples are available in any size or style. Font Harmony, an included program, will resolve ID number conflicts between fonts. Font and Sound Valley, also included, increases disk space by packing various types of files.

Name: **SuperPrint 2.2**
Program type: Font manager
Vendor: Zenographics
Cost: $196
Hardware requirements: IBM compatible; 2MB RAM minimum; 3.5MB disk space
Additional software needed: Windows 3.x
Description: This utility will scale fonts "on-the-fly" for use with Windows. Several modules integrate to perform an excellent interface. SuperText Manager is a typeface-selection tool. SuperQueue is a printer spooler for printing numerous documents in a row. The system does not support PostScript-only printers and does not send PostScript code to a PostScript printer. Twenty-two typefaces are included with the product.
Review source: *PC Computing*, December 1990, 48.

Name: **TypeStyler**
Program type: Font manipulation program
Vendor: Broderbund Software, Inc.
Cost: $199.95; $50 for owners of PosterMaker Plus
Hardware requirements: Macintosh; 1MB RAM minimum; 1.5MB disk storage
Description: TypeStyler is a good program for creating special effects with display type. Typefaces can be bent, squeezed, stretched, twisted, and rotated. The program also can add

perspective, shadows, shades, inlines and outlines, patterns, and colors to text. Ten typefaces are included. Other, third party, fonts can be manipulated for use with the program as well. Data created can be converted into Adobe Illustrator files. PICT and EPS files can be imported and exported. The program can be used to design logos, signage, advertising graphics, newsletters, package art, presentations, and manuals.

Review source: *Apple Library Users Group*, January 1990, 73.

Training Programs

Training programs help users learn about some other program. Some programs, of course, come with their own tutorials, but many either do not have them or have inadequate instructions. Some packages come with the software and an audiotape, while others are video lessons. Training programs can help instill confidence in first-time users.

There are many additional programs available besides those listed in this section. The programs here are representative of such material.

A training program can be only part of the learning process. Users may do well to purchase an additional text or two on their programs for additional assistance and help.

Name:	**Adobe Illustrator**
Program type:	Video training
Vendor:	MacAcademy
Cost:	$49 each (3 videos)
Hardware requirements:	VHS videotape player
Additional software needed:	Adobe Illustrator
Description:	Video 1 covers installation, components, selection tools, rectangle tools, oval tools, pen tools, grouping and ungrouping, paint menu, scaling tool, rotation tool, reflection tool, shearing tool, preferences, curves, and pen tool additional. Video 2 covers opening program, windows, blending tool, make guide, scaling tool, rulers, graph paper, blending points, masking, auto tracing, text, text creation tool, custom colors, custom fonts, and text paths. Video 3 covers separator, densitometer chart, type fonts, Pantone colors, type manager, compound paths, cutting type, type manipulation, blending type, page layouts, custom patterns, and graphs.

Name:	**Adobe Photoshop**
Program type:	Video training
Vendor:	MacAcademy

Cost:	$49 each (4 videos)
Hardware requirements:	VHS videotape player
Additional software needed:	Adobe Photoshop
Description:	This set of four videotapes teaches various aspects of the use of the Adobe Photoshop. Video 1 covers Photoshop preferences, virtual memory, zoom tool, pixel concept, cropping tool, marquee tool, lasso tool, magic wand tool, pixel memory, pen tool, RGB and CYMK modes, eye dropper tool, and rubber stamp tool. Video 2 covers line tool, eraser tool, air brush, text, blur and sharpen, paint bucket, scanning, brightness menu, black-and-white control, color control, level control, and color balance. Video 3 covers channels, color picker, create brush, alpha channel, threshold, copy/paste, text, stroke, transform images, scale, distort filters, printing, and image size. Video 4 covers silhouettes, textures, blur, scaling, inverting image, adjust levels, colorize gray scale, calculate, filters, RGB mode, channels, colorize, and special effects.

Name:	**Aldus FreeHand**
Program type:	Video training
Vendor:	MacAcademy
Cost:	$49 each (3 videos)
Hardware requirements:	VHS videotape player
Additional software needed:	Aldus FreeHand
Description:	Video 1 covers accessory files, using tools, backgrounds, graphics, palettes, defining colors, graphic tools, tints and shadows, rotation tool, grouping and layering, file menu, power duplication, and document setup. Video 2 covers custom colors, removing colors, creating styles, fill effects, type menu, fill menu, text on path, blending, composite graphics, and clipping paths. Video 3 covers layer managers, print specifications, page setup, importing graphics, graphic tricks, blending colors, placing graphics, element information, overprinting, blending paths, and auto trace.
Review source:	*MacWorld*, January 1992, 223.

Name:	**Aldus PageMaker**
Program type:	Video training
Vendor:	MacAcademy
Cost:	$49 each (4 videos)
Hardware requirements:	VHS playback device

Additional software needed: Aldus PageMaker

Description: Video 1 covers desktop publishing tips, installation program, document, page views, insert pages, rulers, column guides, master pages, page numbering, tools, graphics, fill patterns, placing graphics, placing text, and layering. Video 2 covers reverse type, shadow boxes, drop caps, in-line graphics, leading, type width, story editor, pull quotes, find/change, text rotation, paragraph options, spelling check, and preferences. Video 3 covers defaults, templates, linking, style sheets, new styles, image control, text wrap options, color options, tabs/indents, book options, and tips and tricks. Video 4 covers table editor, color, table of contents, new features, booklet edition, column balancing, additions, hot linking to FreeHand, run scripts, printing options, and sort pages.

Name: **Aldus Persuasion**

Program type: Videotape training

Vendor: MacAcademy

Cost: $49 each (2 videos)

Hardware requirements: VHS videotape player

Additional software needed: Aldus Persuasion

Description: Video 1 covers introduction, program installation, creating presentations, auto templates, slide outline, editing text, place holders, background masters, creating and using graphics, creating slide shows, charts and tables, draw tools, text and graphics, printing techniques, and output functions. Video 2 covers layering, formatting, note pages, spelling checker and find/change, altering placeholders, slide master, backgrounds, bullets, auto templates, shortcuts, and using service bureaus.

Name: **Aldus SuperPaint 3.0**

Program type: Videotape training

Vendor: MacAcademy

Cost: $49 each (3 videos)

Hardware requirements: VHS videotape player

Additional software needed: SuperPaint 3.0

Description: Video 1 covers graphics, tools, printing options, paint layer, palettes, patterns, hot keys, paint versus draw, rotation tool, grouping and layering, file menu, hide layer, and text. Video 2 covers line tool, shape tool, custom shapes, polygon tool, freehand tool, text, eye dropper tool, plug-ins, airbrush, masking, painting multiple, and eraser tool. Video 3 covers brush symmetry, trace edges, diffusing, mosaic, reshape objects, Bezier curves, scale drawing, replicate, rotate graphics, gradients, textures, color, and patterns.

Name:	**Claris MacDraw Pro**
Program type:	Video training
Vendor:	MacAcademy
Cost:	$49 each (2 videos)
Hardware requirements:	VHS videotape player
Additional software needed:	MacDraw Pro
Description:	Video 1 covers program, translators, slide show, help, tools, painting, pen tools, color palettes, editing patterns, fills, text, object creation, polygon preferences, arc tool, drawing sizes, Bezier tool, and import/export. Video 2 covers importing charts, eye dropper tool, rulers, grouping, slide presentation, layer management, importing objects, gradient manager, editing colors, importing text, note tool, text ruler, EPS file, libraries, gradients, and drawing order.

Name:	**ClarisWorks**
Program type:	Video training
Vendor:	MacAcademy
Cost:	$49 each (4 videos)
Hardware requirements:	VHS videotape player
Additional software needed:	ClarisWorks
Description:	Video 1 covers word processing: program, components, document window, text ruler, menus, on-line help, formatting, color, tabs, line spacing, spelling check, find/change, columns, footnotes, headers/footers, and printing. Video 2 covers spreadsheets: environment, formatting, design, color, number format, formulas, charting, sorting, single criterion sort, protection, relative cell address, functions, logic functions, checks, and macros. Video 3 covers database topics: database, defining fields, menus, page set-up, new records, duplicating records, sorting, find, additional fields, new layout, importing graphics, zoom control, align objects, tab order, calculations, and columnar reports. Video 4 covers graphics: creating objects, text tool, spreadsheet frame, graphics tools, grouping, reshaping, importing graphics,

newsletter, multiple pages, linking text, integrating, graphs, archiving database, mail merge, communications, and sending a file.

Name:	**dBase IV (Teach Yourself . . .)**
Program type:	Training
Vendor:	American Training International
Cost:	$74.95
Hardware requirements:	IBM compatible; Macintosh; 128KB RAM minimum
Additional software needed:	dBase IV
Description:	This is an easy-to-use program for learning the fundamentals of dBase IV.

Name:	**Deneba Canvas 3.0**
Program type:	Video training
Vendor:	MacAcademy
Cost:	$49 each (3 videos)
Hardware requirements:	VHS videotape player
Additional software needed:	Canvas 3.0
Description:	Video 1 covers basic tools and palettes, multiplex tools, menus and preferences, object (drawing) and bitmap (painting) concerns, grouping and locking objects; drawing order: shuffling, paste priorities; Bezier curves: creating and editing, setting defaults, patterns sets, and foreground and background color use. Video 2 covers working with text: creation and modification, text on paths (encrusting, slanting, scaling); creating and manipulating text outlines, text rulers (tabs, formatting, leading); spell checking; special edit managers and tools; duplication of objects; auto tracing; layers and the layer manager; use of Pantone colors. Video 3 covers multiple object transformations, gradient fills (use and creation), blending objects, combining and slicing objects, creation and presentation slide shows, dimensioning drawings, use of hatch (cross-section) patterns, separations for printing or negatives, and the Macintosh operating system—System 7.0—special options (publish and subscribe).

Name:	**Design and Layout Techniques for Desktop Publishers**
Program type:	Video training
Vendor:	MacAcademy
Cost:	$49

Hardware requirements: VHS videotape player

Description: The video provides a general overview of desktop publishing, design, and layout. It describes and illustrates design options, planning documents, font options, readability, using graphics, grids and columns, moderation, clip art, logos, proofing, scanners, image setting, color options, printing options, and desktop publishing help.

Name: **Desktop Design**

Program type: Video training

Vendor: Step-by-Step Video

Cost: $39.95

Hardware requirements: VHS videotape player

Description: The videotape program gives basic training in generic applications and design work.

Name: **DOS 5.0 (Teach Yourself . . .)**

Program type: Training

Vendor: American Training International

Cost: $49.95

Hardware requirements: IBM compatible; 360KB floppy or hard disk drive

Additional software needed: DOS 5.0

Description: The program helps users pick up basic DOS skills. It loads directly to hard drive or floppy for easy execution.

Name: **Font Management for the Macintosh**

Program type: Videotape training

Vendor: MacAcademy

Cost: $49

Hardware requirements: VHS videotape player

Description: Macintosh users can get an excellent understanding of fonts and their use by watching this tape. It covers system resources, system file, system folder, screen fonts, printer fonts, PostScript fonts, installing TrueType fonts, finding printer fonts, identifying installed fonts.

Name: **IBM PC, XT, AT (How to Use Your . . .)**

Program type: Training

Vendor: American Training International

Cost: $49.95

Hardware requirements: IBM compatible; 64KB RAM minimum; 360KB floppy or hard disk drive

Description: The program gives fundamental instruction on the use of an IBM-compatible computer.

Name: **JAZ Computer Tutor Series**
Program type: Video training
Vendor: Library Video Company
Cost: $119.80 set; $29.95 each (4 videos)
Hardware requirements: VHS videotape player
Description: Four separate tapes cover the fundamentals of computers, DOS, Lotus 1-2-3, and WordPerfect.

Name: **Lotus 1-2-3**
Program type: Video training
Vendor: MacAcademy
Cost: $49 each (3 videos)
Hardware requirements: VHS videotape player
Additional software needed: Lotus 1-2-3
Description: Video 1 covers cells, components, text, formulas, templates, print options, format, styles, publishing, relative references, menus, and color. Video 2 covers text box, tools, @ functions, payment function, graphs, charts, backsolve, menus, display options, and fill. Video 3 covers data menu, what-if table, matrix, sorting, database, macros, linking, find, buttons, references, query, and subroutines.

Name: **Lotus 1-2-3 3.1 (Teach Yourself . . .)**
Program type: Training
Vendor: American Training International
Cost: $74.95
Hardware requirements: IBM compatible; 64KB RAM minimum; 360KB floppy or hard disk drive
Additional software needed: Lotus 1-2-3
Description: The program loads easily to hard drive for execution. Users gain instruction in the fundamental aspects of Lotus 1-2-3.

Name: **Microsoft Word 5.0 (Teach Yourself . . .)**
Program type: Training
Vendor: American Training International
Cost: $74.95
Hardware requirements: IBM compatible; 64KB RAM minimum
Additional software needed: Microsoft Word 5.0

Description: User gains elementary knowledge of word processing skills necessary for Microsoft Word.

Name: **Microsoft Word 5.0**
Program type: Video training
Vendor: MacAcademy
Cost: $49 each (4 videos)
Hardware requirements: VHS videotape player
Additional software needed: Microsoft Word
Description: Four videotapes present various aspects of the Microsoft Word word-processing system. Video 1 covers word processing, style options, documents, keyboard shortcuts, spelling checker, grammar checker, ruler, menus, and tabs. Video 2 covers paragraphs, tab leaders, formatting, tables, mail merge, mailing labels, inserting graphics, and voice annotations. Video 3 covers headers and footers, table of contents, index, footnotes, outlining, glossary, and publish and subscribe. Video 4 covers embedding objects, new features, find and replace, file management, mail merge, and custom styles.

Name: **Paints & Draws**
Program type: Video training
Vendor: MacAcademy
Cost: $49
Hardware requirements: VHS videotape player
Description: The program gives a good overview of software available for printing and drawing as well as how to use tool palettes, create graphics, screen dumps, clipboard, group graphics, paint and draw special effects, and proof prints.

Name: **Paradox (Teach Yourself . . .)**
Program type: Training
Vendor: American Training International
Cost: $74.95
Hardware requirements: IBM compatible; 128KB RAM minimum; 360KB floppy or hard disk drive
Additional software needed: Paradox
Description: This easy-to-use program loads onto the hard drive or a floppy with a few simple keystrokes. It provides instruction on the use of basic functions of Paradox.

Name: **Personal Training Systems**
Program type: Training
Vendor: Personal Training Systems
Cost: Inquire, not available at press time
Hardware requirements: Macintosh
Description: The system has many modules available for major computer programs with beginning, intermediate, and advanced levels. Each set contains a 90-minute audiocassette, disk for hands-on, step-by-step tutorial, command summary card, and a practice card. Available for FreeHand, Illustrator, PageMaker, Persuasion, Microsoft Works, Lotus 1-2-3, QuarkXPress, and WordPerfect.

Name: **QuarkXPress**
Program type: Video training
Vendor: MacAcademy
Cost: $49 each (3 videos)
Hardware requirements: VHS videotape player
Additional software needed: QuarkXPress
Description: Video 1 covers installation, organization, guides, text box, graphic box, format text, color text, tracking, graphics, text, blend, and layout. Video 2 covers library, poster, save, text runaround, paragraph format, drop caps, color, scan image, columns, master pages, rotation tool, and style sheets. Video 3 covers rulers, reverse type, trapping, tabs, document layout, placing text, page numbers, section numbers, baseline grid, in-line graphics, tracking table, graphic styles, and printing.

Name: **R:Base 5000 (Teach Yourself . . .)**
Program type: Training
Vendor: American Training International
Cost: $74.95
Hardware requirements: IBM compatible; 128KB RAM minimum; 360KB floppy or hard disk
Additional software needed: R:Base 5000
Description: This tutorial makes it much easier to learn the basic operation of this database system. It is excellent for beginning users.

Name: **R:Base System V (Teach Yourself . . .)**
Program type: Training
Vendor: American Training International

Cost:	$74.95
Hardware requirements:	IBM compatible; 128KB RAM minimum; 360KB floppy or hard drive
Additional software needed:	R:Base System V
Description:	The easy-to-use program can be loaded directly to hard disk drive with a simple command. It is excellent for beginners who want to quickly pick up the basic skills of this database management system.

Name:	**Symphony Learning System**
Program type:	Training
Vendor:	MicroVideo Learning Systems
Cost:	$595
Hardware requirements:	IBM compatible
Description:	This learning package for Symphony contains material for learning to use the word processor, spreadsheet, database, graphs, and telecommunications. It also covers macros, data exchange, and more.

Name:	**Video Professor Series**
Program type:	Video training
Vendor:	Video Professor
Cost:	$19.95 each
Hardware requirements:	VHS videotape player
Description:	This is an excellent series of tutorial software. The set contains: Introduction to Ventura, Introduction to PFS: First Publisher, Introduction to PFS: First Choice, PFS: First Choice II, PFS: First Choice III, and Introduction to WordPerfect.

Name:	**Wind-Ease**
Program type:	Training
Vendor:	Black Orchid Software, Inc.
Cost:	$49
Hardware requirements:	IBM compatible
Additional software needed:	Windows
Description:	The program provides hands-on training in most key concepts of Microsoft Windows 3.0.

Name:	**WordPerfect Companion**
Program type:	Training
Vendor:	Eastern Digital Resources
Cost:	$15

Hardware requirements:	IBM compatible; 640KB RAM minimum; 1.5MB disk space
Additional software needed:	WordPerfect
Description:	This training program is for use with WordPerfect. It gives useful advice, tips, and training. The price is right.

Name:	**WordPerfect 5.1 (Teach Yourself . . .)**
Program type:	Training
Vendor:	American Training International
Cost:	$74.95
Hardware requirements:	IBM compatible; 128KB RAM minimum
Additional software needed:	WordPerfect 5.1
Description:	This easy-to-use program provides practice with Word-Perfect program commands.

Programs for Use by or with Children

School and children's librarians often are looking for products to use with students. Most of the programs in this section differ from other programs listed in this book only in that they are simpler to use or that they have some cartoon theme that makes them more appealing to children.

Some programs listed here also can be used by librarians and other educators to create materials for library or classroom use or distribution.

Name: **Babydraw**
Program type: Drawing program for children
Vendor: Software Labs
Cost: $3.69 (shareware)
Hardware requirements: IBM compatible (color graphics required)
Description: This drawing program for children turns the screen and keyboard into an entertaining and learning experience. Sound effects, graphics, and colors change with each keystroke. Even children as young as 2 years old can have fun keying in their favorite color. Beyond the cause and effect mode, Babydraw can be used by older children to learn the elementary steps in drawing and painting. Features include draw, edit, fill colors, change background colors, change palette, display grids, save, and print drawings. Online help is available.

Name: **Beauty and the Beast Print Kit**
Program type: Print kit
Vendor: Walt Disney Computer Software, Inc.
Cost: $19.95
Hardware requirements: IBM compatible
Description: Based on the popular recent film, the program provides a variety of graphics for creating colorful and interesting products such as calendars, invitations, diaries, book-

marks, etc. Children will love working with the characters from the film to create their own displays.

Name:	**Big & Little**
Program type:	Poster maker
Vendor:	Sunburst Communications, Inc.
Cost:	$59 (single user); $236 (network)
Hardware requirements:	Apple II series; 128KB RAM: 5.25- or 3.5-inch disk
Additional software needed:	Muppet Slate
Description:	Big & Little is an easy-to-use program that allows students to create their own small cards or large posters up to six feet tall. Children can also create their own books. It is not designed to be used alone, but with Muppet Slate, a program that processes words and pictures.

Name:	**Cartooners**
Program type:	Storybook creation for children
Vendor:	Electronic Arts
Cost:	$24.95
Hardware requirements:	IBM compatible; 512KB RAM minimum
Description:	This entertaining program provides creative opportunities for children of any age. Users create their own printed, illustrated storybooks in full color.

Name:	**Cotton Tales**
Program type:	Desktop publishing for children
Vendor:	Mindscape
Cost:	$49.99; $129 (Lab Pack)
Hardware requirements:	Apple II; IBM compatible; Macintosh
Additional software available:	Cotton Works contains fifty individually prepared worksheets with lessons for grades K to 2 on labeling, sorting, sequencing, division, multiplication, etc. Cotton Plus is a library of 160 graphics.
Description:	This extremely simple-to-use program is for grades pre-K to 3. Its basic features and skills include word processing (insert, erase, copy, save, and print), developing basic reading skills, creating picture stories, and improving spelling skills.

Name:	**816/Paint Education**
Program type:	Draw/paint
Vendor:	Baudville Computer Products
Cost:	$125

Hardware requirements:	Apple II family
Description:	This program differs from 816/Paint in the additional materials provided for classroom use. This is the perfect paint program for use with students. It contains thirty-eight classroom activities, seven reproducible student handouts, and twenty student-user manuals.

Name:	**KidMaps**
Program type:	Map clip art for use with children
Vendor:	MicroMaps
Cost:	$16
Hardware requirements:	Macintosh
Additional software needed:	KidPix, SuperPaint, or Canvas
Description:	The collection of maps was created specifically for use by children. Special tools let them create and change the image in their own way.

Name:	**Kid Pix**
Program type:	Creativity program for children
Vendor:	Broderbund Software, Inc.
Cost:	$31
Hardware requirements:	Macintosh
Description:	Kid Pix is a spectacular paint program that brings computer creativity to children ages 3 and up. They can easily master the tools to create many simple documents. Users may record greetings, poems, or music. On top of being easy to use and useful, Kid Pix is also fun to use. The system uses a WYSIWYG format. Drawing tools obviously for children include Wacky Pencil (draws irregular or "wacky" lines), Truck (cut and paste), Rubber Stamp (copy utility), Text tool (copy letters utility), and Eraser. Pictures are saved in either PICT or MacPaint format. Material can be exported to many programs including PageMaker.

Name:	**Mickey's Crossword Puzzle Maker**
Program type:	Puzzle maker
Vendor:	Walt Disney Computer Software, Inc.
Cost:	$39.95 (Apple II); $49.95 (IBM)
Hardware requirements:	Apple II series; IBM compatible
Description:	This simple and easy-to-use program allows children to prepare original puzzles. Instructions are contained on-line. Children are apt to be entertained since the Disney

characters appear on screen, as does a fireworks display. Their favorite cartoon characters can be edited into the puzzles: Goofy, Pluto, Donald, Mickey, etc. It also contains a game-playing option. The program will play twenty familiar tunes.

Name: **Muppets Print Kit**
Program type: Print kit
Vendor: Hi Tech Expressions
Cost: $14.95
Hardware requirements: IBM compatible; 256KB RAM
Description: This program is similar to others listed here but with a focus on the Muppet characters. It can be used to create stationery, banners, puppets, masks, and to write and illustrate Muppet stories.

Name: **Picture Perfect**
Program type: Educational graphics package
Vendor: Mindplay
Cost: $49.99; $129 (lab pack of 6 copies and 2 users' manuals)
Hardware requirements: Apple II with either joystick or Applemouse; IBM compatible with CGA graphics card and joystick; Epson, Imagewriter, Grappler +, Pkaso, or Silentype printer
Description: Intended for use with pre-K to grade 6 students, the program helps children express themselves with this graphics, story-design package by making coloring books and storybooks. A variety of functions introduce users to freehand drawing (including brush strokes and five color choices for fill patterns) with line, point, connected line, fill, and box. A collection of 84 graphics is included. These can be moved, stretched, or flipped. Text can be added to pictures when necessary. The finished product can be sent to a printer.

Name: **Professional Sign Maker**
Program type: Banner and sign maker
Vendor: Sunburst Communications, Inc.
Cost: $65, single disk, or $195 lab pack of ten; $260 Corvus Network version
Hardware requirements: Apple II family
Description: The program can be used by educators or students to create signs, advertisements, report covers, etc.

Name:	**VCR Companion**
Program type:	Videotape titles and credit maker
Vendor:	Broderbund Software, Inc.
Cost:	$59.95; $64.95 (school edition with backup disks and Teacher's Guide; $129.95 (lab pack)
Hardware requirements:	IBM compatible with composite video output
Additional software available:	VCR Companion Film Library ($24.95) contains 120 design elements, including 20 animations, 20 full-screen images, 24 icon elements, 12 fonts, etc.
Description:	For librarians or individuals creating their own videotape productions, this program will help make videos look more professional. Credits, titles, transitions, introductions, and special effects can be added in color. Six ready-made sequences are included. All can be customized according to needs. Mix-and-match designs from a selection of 120 graphics, fonts, borders, animations, and icons can be used. The program is very easy to use and is similar in concept to Print Shop. When production elements are finished, they are transferred to videotape. An alternative to the use of a VCR is to make a self-booting "FilmDisks."

Name:	**The Writing Center**
Program type:	Word Processor with some desktop publishing features
Vendor:	The Learning Company
Cost:	$89.95 ($129.95 for institutions)
Hardware requirements:	Macintosh
Description:	A graphics and text package, The Writing Center is designed for use with students ages 7 and up. Its library of images includes 220 color clip art pieces including animals, science, nature, history, school, holidays, sports, food, people, etc. The program will allow for PICT images anywhere on the page. Layouts may contain one, two, or custom columns. Despite its apparent ease of use and capability, it has many limitations that make it inadequate for high-level word processing or graphic production. It is excellent, however, for teaching students the concepts of word processing and desktop publishing. It can also be used in any situation in which only simple products are needed.
Review source:	*MacWorld*, January 1992, 175.

Clip Art and Template Collections

Clip art is prepackaged artwork that can be transferred to a desktop publishing program or graphics package. It is a way of avoiding drawing things from scratch. There is an enormous number of images available. The cost of a clip art package does not often give a clue to its quality, since very inexpensive shareware and public domain clip art costs only three or four dollars per disk. Commercially available clip art can easily cost ten times that and not be nearly as good.

There are two general types of clip art: line drawings with no shading (outlines) and complete artwork with shading.

It is interesting to see the variety of the offerings. While not all will be useful to librarians, there is certainly enough for any type of library, including clip art depicting sports, religion, holidays, and much more.

All clip art comes in a format. When possible, the formats for the files have been given below (e.g., WPG).

A good source book for Macintosh clip art is Erfert Fenton's *Canned Art: Clip Art for the Macintosh* (Emeryville, Calif.: Peachpit Press, 1991). This volume contains sources for more than 15,000 pieces of clip art. Additional information such as format, utilities, and clip art management is also included.

Name:	**Accents & Borders 1**
Program type:	Clip art for newsletters and flyers
Vendor:	3-D Graphics
Cost:	$64
Hardware requirements:	Macintosh
Additional software needed:	Any program that uses PostScript format
Description:	The package contains a variety of exciting borders for use with many pamphlet, flyer, or poster productions. It also comes with many small labels, symbols, and other items to accent pages in many ways. These include materials for holidays and events, people, food, and much more.

Name:	**Adobe Collector's Edition I: Symbols, Borders & Letters**
Program type:	Clip art
Vendor:	Adobe Systems, Inc.

Cost:	$125
Hardware requirements:	Macintosh; 1MB RAM minimum
Additional software needed:	Adobe Illustrator or similar drawing program
Description:	The package contains a useful selection of 100 borders and 300 dingbat elements for use with Adobe Illustrator.

Name:	**Adobe Collector's Edition II: Patterns & Textures**
Program type:	Clip art
Vendor:	Adobe Systems, Inc.
Cost:	$225
Hardware requirements:	Macintosh
Additional software needed:	Adobe Illustrator or similar drawing program
Description:	The package contains a useful selection of more than 400 different texture and pattern designs for use with Adobe Illustrator.

Name:	**AHOY PCX**
Program type:	Clip art
Vendor:	Software Labs
Cost:	$3.69; $4.69 for 3.5-inch format
Hardware requirements:	IBM compatible
Additional software needed:	Any program that accepts PCX graphics
Description:	The program contains ten exciting graphics of scanned images (line drawings of woodcuts) of antique sailing vessels. It includes cruise ships and ocean-going vessels of the 1700s.

Name:	**Animal PCX Graphics**
Program type:	Clip art
Vendor:	Software Labs
Cost:	$3.69 per disk; $4.69 for 3.5-inch format
Hardware requirements:	IBM compatible
Additional software needed:	Any program that uses PCX graphics
Description:	A large variety of animals is contained within these many disks. Order by individual disk number. 6127: dogs; 6128: cats; 6129: cold-weather animals; 6130: farm animals; 6131: wild animals; 6132: birds; 6133: more birds; 6134: still more birds; 6198: animals; 6199: bats, raptors, bat faces, buzzards, condor, horned owl; 6200: reptiles; 6201: ten animals—badger, coatimundi, ibex, pangolin, wolverine, bison, lynx, cottontail, peccary, skunk; 6202: five more animals—bears, porcupines, rats, vampire bats, hare; 6203: eight animals—beaver, jerboa, spotted ground squirrel, squirrel, wolverine, chimpanzee, mar-

moset, shrew; 6204: ten birds; 6205: seven birds; 6206: eight birds of prey; 6207: six wading birds; 6208: seven waterfowl

Name:	**Art Gallery I, II**
Program type:	Clip art
Vendor:	Unison World Software
Cost:	$39.95
Hardware requirements:	IBM compatible
Additional software needed:	Graphics program
Description:	The program's 140 graphic images can enhance the usefulness of Unison World's PrintMaster, PrintMaster Plus, NewsMaster, and NewsMaster II.

Name:	**Art Portfolio**
Program type:	Clip art
Vendor:	TimeWorks, Inc.
Cost:	$119.95
Hardware requirements:	IBM compatible
Additional software needed:	Publish It! or Publish It Lite!
Description:	The program contains four separate portfolios: Design Ideas (85 layout templates for newsletters, brochures, etc.), Education Graphics (200 graphics), People, Places, and Things (240 graphics), and Symbols and Slogans (450 graphics).

Name:	**Art Library I**
Program type:	Clip art
Vendor:	Melody Hall
Cost:	$9.95
Hardware requirements:	IBM compatible
Additional software needed:	Printware
Description:	This collection of print art contains 75 illustrations of food, people, sports, animals, office equipment, and household items.

Name:	**Art Library II**
Program type:	Clip art
Vendor:	Melody Hall
Cost:	$9.95
Hardware requirements:	IBM compatible
Additional software needed:	Printware

Description: This collection of clip art contains 75 additional illustrations of international flags and symbols, ornament letters, and others.

Name: **Border Clip Art for Libraries**
Program type: Clip art
Vendor: LEI, Inc.
Cost: $49
Hardware requirements: Macintosh
Additional software needed: PageMaker; Ready, Set, Go; Word; or other Mac applications that support EPSF graphics
Description: The package contains 75 computer border graphics, 44 clip art illustrations. All are provided in Encapsulated PostScript Format. The program comes with a discount coupon for The Curator, which will convert graphics for use to MacPaint, TIFF, PICT, or IBM EPSF.

Name: **Business 1**
Program type: Clip art
Vendor: 3-D Graphics
Cost: $64
Hardware requirements: Macintosh
Additional software needed: Any program that uses PostScript format
Description: The program contains pictures of work-related objects and activities such as briefcases, people running to catch a flight, pencils and notepads, etc. Also included is a variety of public symbols, computers, and even phrases.

Name: **ClickArt**
Program type: Clip art
Vendor: T/Maker Co.
Cost: (see each portfolio in description)
Hardware requirements: Macintosh; IBM compatible
Additional software needed: Desktop publishers that use PCX, MSP, IMG, EPS, or MAC file formats; Windows versions require Windows 3.x
Description: This series of clip art packages includes separate sets for business, personal graphics, holidays, publications, etc. The art and images are of high quality. Also noteworthy is the large number of images included—3,000—that cover many subjects. Each portfolio must be ordered separately. The specific portfolios for PostScript images are business, illustrations, animals and nature, sports and games, and

symbols and industry. Specific portfolios for bitmapped portfolios are business cartoons, business images, Christian images, events and holiday cartoons, holidays, personal graphics, and publications. Titles are Artistry and Borders ($129.95), Business Cartoons ($59.95), Business Cartoons for Windows ($59.95), Business Images ($59.95), Business Images for Windows ($59.95), Christian Images ($59.95), Christian Images for Windows ($59.95), Color Graphics for Presentations for Windows ($149.95), Color Graphics for Presentations ($149.95), EPS Animals and Nature ($129.95), Animals and Nature for Windows ($129.95), EPS Business Art ($129.95), EPS Business Art for Windows ($129.95), EPS Illustrations ($129.95), EPS Illustrations for Windows ($129.95), EPS Sports and Games ($129.95), EPS Sports and Games for Windows ($129.95), EPS Symbols and Industry ($129.95), EPS Symbols and Industry for Windows ($129.95), Events and Holiday Cartoons ($59.95), Events and Holiday Cartoons for Windows ($59.95), Holidays ($59.95), Holidays for Windows ($59.95), Newsletter Cartoons ($59.95), Newsletter Cartoons for Windows ($59.95), Personal Graphics ($59.95), Personal Graphics for Windows ($59.95), Publications ($59.95), Publications for Windows ($59.95).

Name:	**ClickArt Scrapbook +**
Program type:	Clip organizer for Windows
Vendor:	T/Maker Co.
Cost:	$129.95
Hardware requirements:	IBM compatible
Additional software needed:	Microsoft Windows
Description:	The Scrapbook + is an organizer for clip art. Images of clip art or text are stored in a clipboard from which they may be retrieved for use in any document. It supports multiple formats: MSP, EPS, PS, RTF, DIF, SLK, WMF, TXT, CSV, and TIFF. This is an especially useful program for users with many images to swap between documents.
Review source:	*PC Magazine*, October 17, 1989, 178.

Name:	**Click & Clip**
Program type:	Clip art
Vendor:	Studio Advertising Art

Cost: $395 for clip art library; $125 annually (also available quarterly for $39.95)

Hardware requirements: Macintosh; IBM compatible

Additional software needed: Desktop publishing or drawing program that uses EPS files

Description: The package contains 500 images in its basic library. Quarterly updates include additional artwork for EPS format that can be used with PageMaker and Ventura Publisher. Images can be edited using a drawing program that handles EPS files.

Review source: *PC Magazine*, October 17, 1989, 168.

Name: **Cliptures**

Program type: PostScript clip art

Vendor: Dream Maker Software

Cost: $129.95 each (4 volumes)

Hardware requirements: Macintosh; IBM compatible; PostScript-compatible printer

Additional software needed: Any program that uses EPS clip art

Description: Four collections contain hundreds of professional clip art: Business (vol. 1) contains 148 images of skylines, calculators, and other business related illustrations. Business 2 (vol. 2) contains 206 additional images of people working, telephones, computers, etc. Sports (vol. 3) contains 228 images of athletes in motion with basketballs, footballs, weight-lifting equipment, etc. World Flags (vol. 4) has excellent representations of flags from all countries of the world, as well as organization and code flags. All are high resolution images created using Adobe Illustrator.

Name: **Color PCX Frames**

Program type: Clip art

Vendor: Software Labs

Cost: $3.69; $4.69 in 3.5-inch format

Hardware requirements: IBM compatible

Additional software needed: Any software package that accepts PCX format

Description: Frames can be used for signs, posters, and flyers. The collection of 23 frames contains exciting and dramatic use of clowns, dragons, beer glass and keg, Queen Victoria, jet, cowardly lion, and more. Each leaves central space for a message and uses color graphics.

Name: **The Curator**
Program type: Art manager
Vendor: Solutions International
Cost: $139.95
Hardware requirements: Macintosh
Description: This program operates as a graphics librarian by keeping track of artwork in a table of contents that contains miniature pictures (thumbnails), names, and keywords. All artwork, however, remains in its original format. The Curator also will make incompatible artwork formats (e.g., TIFF, Encapsulated PostScript, PICT, Glue, PostScript, and MacPaint) compatible. When using a graphic, The Curator can be used to do a Save As command to create the correct format. It reads PictureBase files.

Name: **Design Ideas**
Program type: Clip art
Vendor: TimeWorks, Inc.
Cost: $39.95
Hardware requirements: IBM compatible
Additional software needed: Publish It! or Publish It Lite!
Description: The set contains 85 design and layout plans for creating brochures, newsletters, invitations, catalogs, ads, and more.

Name: **Education Graphics**
Program type: Clip art
Vendor: TimeWorks, Inc.
Cost: $39.95
Hardware requirements: IBM compatible
Additional software needed: Publish It!
Description: As its name implies, the program contains 200 graphics for use in educational settings.

Name: **FaxMania**
Program type: Template collection for use as fax covers
Vendor: T/Maker Company
Cost: $69.95
Hardware requirements: Macintosh
Description: This is a set of 80 fax cover sheet templates for business or home use. The set contains messages that are serious

(e.g., urgent) and those that are flippant (Don't have a cow man!).

Name:	**Full Page Images Library**
Program type:	Full-page clip art
Vendor:	Artbeats
Cost:	$59 (CD-ROM versions available for $229 for each of two volumes)
Hardware requirements:	Macintosh
Additional software needed:	EPS software
Description:	The program provides complete backgrounds for many different types of publications, including posters and newsletters.

Name:	**Gallery Effects: Texture Art**
Program type:	Texture clip art
Vendor:	Aldus Corp.
Cost:	$199
Hardware requirements:	Macintosh
Description:	The package contains 125 textures grouped by categories such as marble, wood, stone, metal, fabric, etc.

Name:	**Graphics & Symbols 1**
Program type:	Clip art
Vendor:	3-D Graphics
Cost:	$55
Hardware requirements:	Macintosh
Additional software needed:	Any program that uses PostScript format
Description:	This excellent set of images includes people running and playing, food, travel, symbols, and even some cartoons.

Name:	**Graphics Pak**
Program type:	Clip art
Vendor:	Artware Systems, Inc.
Cost:	$149.95
Hardware requirements:	Macintosh; 12MB disk space
Additional software needed:	Any program that uses EPS format
Description:	The file consists of approximately 300 line images of animals, holidays, people, office workers, borders, etc.

Name:	**Grin Graphics**
Program type:	Clip art cartoon characters
Vendor:	Software Labs

Cost:	$3.69 per disk; $4.69 for 3.5-inch format
Hardware requirements:	IBM compatible
Additional software needed:	Graphics program
Description:	Each set contains two diskettes of clip art of 158 cartoon characters in funny and amusing positions and situations that include animals, people, etc. Includes graphic format information. Two diskettes for each of the following: PCX, ART, BMP, TIF, WPG, GIF, IMG, LBM.

Name:	**International Symbols and Signs-N-Symbols for PCX 1.6**
Program type:	Clip art
Vendor:	Studio Advertising Art
Cost:	$99
Hardware requirements:	Macintosh; IBM compatible; 512KB RAM minimum; 1.5MB disk space
Additional software needed:	Any software package that accepts PCX format
Description:	This is two collections in one. International Symbols contains 42 items that include: No parking, phone, stairs, men's room, women's room, first aid, exit, no entry, no smoking, taxi/bus, coffee shop, no dogs, gifts, fire extinguishers, waiting room, water fountain, mail, and many others. Signs-N-Symbols contains 78 items, including astrological and international symbols and Smokey the bear.

Name:	**Library Clip Art**
Program type:	Clip art
Vendor:	LEI, Inc.
Cost:	$214.27 for four volumes (also available in print form for $124.95)
Hardware requirements:	IBM compatible; Macintosh
Description:	The package contains hundreds of library- and school-related images. Books are a big highlight: people sitting at desks reading, carrying piles of books, etc.

Name:	**Library of Clip Art Disk Version Complete**
Program type:	Clip art
Vendor:	LEI, Inc.
Cost:	$214.27; $53.57 for seasons category
Hardware requirements:	Macintosh; IBM compatible
Additional software needed:	Specify format when ordering: PC EPSF, PCX, Mac EPSF, and Paint.

Description: This large graphic collection contains images in the following categories: libraries and reading, bookmobile, senior citizens, holidays and seasonal events, book sales, craft fairs, children's services, A-V materials, periodicals, and reference. Additional artwork is available for the four seasons.

Name: **MacGallery Bit-Mapped Clip Art**
Program type: Clip art
Vendor: Dream Maker Software
Cost: $49.95
Hardware requirements: Macintosh; 1.2MB disk space
Additional software needed: MacPaint
Description: The program contains good quality clip art of many images appropriate for library children's publications and newsletters. It includes holiday settings.

Name: **MapArt: Presentation Quality Clip Art Maps**
Program type: Clip art
Vendor: MicroMap Software
Cost: $89 per version; $95 for CD-ROM (contains both versions)
Hardware requirements: Macintosh; 2MB RAM minimum
Additional software needed: Desktop publishing program
Description: Three separate versions of this program are available. MapArt EPS supports programs such as Adobe Illustrator or Freehand. Another, MapArt PICT, supports PICT files for MacDraw, Canvas, or MacDraft. Both sets, plus one for Paint, are available as a CD-ROM collection. All contain 4 world maps, 12 regional maps with borders of countries, and 24 maps of states and provinces.

Name: **Modern Art**
Program type: Clip art
Vendor: Logitech, Inc.
Cost: $39 each (5 packages)
Hardware requirements: IBM compatible
Additional software needed: Any desktop publisher or word processor that uses TIF, PCX, IMG, EPS, MSP, or BMP formats
Description: Five separate packages contain more than 100 images each, all scanned at 300 dots per inch. The packages are Business and Professional; Newsletters, Symbols and Borders; Holiday and Special Occasion; Sports, Recrea-

tion and Travel; and People, Places and Things. Each set works with PageMaker, Microsoft Word, Ventura Publisher, PFS: First Publisher, and other programs.

Name:	**Office Pictures**
Program type:	Clip art
Vendor:	Software Labs
Cost:	$3.69 per disk; $4.69 for 3.5-inch format
Hardware requirements:	IBM compatible
Additional software needed:	Ventura Publisher or other desktop package that uses IMG (GEM) format
Description:	Pictures of 100 office scenes of people talking on a telephone, working at a desk, etc., are in this package. Custom message areas are contained in many of the graphics.

Name:	**PagePak**
Program type:	Business templates
Vendor:	Imageline, Inc.
Cost:	$99
Hardware requirements:	Macintosh; IBM compatible
Additional software needed:	Microsoft Word or Word Perfect; draw and paint program
Description:	The program contains 50 page designs that, when manipulated with a draw or paint program and edited with Microsoft Word or WordPerfect, result in high level finished newsletters, proposals, manuals, reports, forms, brochures, etc. The program will save the inexperienced user much time in creating complex pages using headlines, text, and graphics. Graphics can be imported from clip art programs.

Name:	**People at Leisure and People in Business**
Program type:	Clip art
Vendor:	Educorp
Cost:	$149.95 each
Hardware requirements:	Macintosh; 5MB RAM minimum; CD-ROM Drive
Additional software needed:	Any desktop publisher that uses PostScript clip art
Description:	These two packages include settings of many people at work and play. Areas include industry (with 75 occupational symbols), healthcare (hospital and clinic settings), etc. People are seen using office equipment, etc. The leisure collection contains fitness, sports, arts, entertainment, and other activities. Most are energetic portrayals,

some are humorous. The images are appropriate for a variety of flyers, newsletters, posters, etc.

Name:	**People, Places & Things**
Program type:	Clip art
Vendor:	TimeWorks, Inc.
Cost:	$39.95
Hardware requirements:	IBM compatible
Additional software needed:	Publish It! or Publish It Lite!
Description:	The package contains 240 illustrations of objects (tools, etc.), places (e.g., the Eiffel Tower), and people.

Name:	**PFS First Publisher Art #1**
Program type:	Clip art maps
Vendor:	Software Labs
Cost:	$3.69
Hardware requirements:	IBM compatible
Additional software needed:	PFS First Publisher
Description:	This disk of map art in ART format includes North America, Canada, Hawaii, Central and South America, Australia, Caribbean Islands, the North Pole, and the Middle East.

Name:	**PFS First Publisher Art #2**
Program type:	Clip art
Vendor:	Software Labs
Cost:	$3.69
Hardware requirements:	IBM compatible
Additional software needed:	PFS First Publisher
Description:	The program in ART format has more than 200 graphics that include objects, characters, animals, symbols, signs, and people.

Name:	**PFS First Publisher Library #1**
Program type:	Clip art
Vendor:	Software Labs
Cost:	$3.69
Hardware requirements:	IBM compatible
Additional software needed:	PFS First Publisher
Description:	These 700 small cartoons can be used to spice up any newsletter or flyer. The package contains people, animals, objects, picture frames, and ready-made signs in ART format.

Name: **PicturePaks 1, 2, and 3**

Program type: Clip art

Vendor: Imageline, Inc.

Cost: $99 (each library)

Hardware requirements: Macintosh; IBM compatible

Additional software needed: Any software package that uses EPS or PICT2 files

Description: The separate libraries of images include the following categories: executive and management, federal government edition, state and local government edition, U.S. maps and landmarks edition, sales and marketing, and finance and administration. The graphic images for these business topics are very simple, usually either in outline or silhouette form. Office environments, such as people at desks or blackboards, and finance dominate these drawings. They can be used for many types of advertising.

Review source: *PC Magazine*, October 17, 1989, 217.

Name: **Plants and Trees**

Program type: Clip art

Vendor: Software Labs

Cost: $3.69; $4.69 for 3.5-inch format

Hardware requirements: IBM compatible

Additional software needed: Any program that accepts PCX graphics

Description: This collection of 25 graphics of trees and plants is in PCX format. Images include acorns, mushrooms, acacia trees, avocados, almonds, orchids, dogwood, California poppies, violets, pampas grass, and more.

Name: **Print Shop Deluxe Sampler Graphics Collection**

Program type: Clip art

Vendor: Broderbund Software, Inc.

Cost: $44.95

Hardware requirements: IBM compatible: 1MB disk space

Additional software needed: Print Shop Deluxe

Description: The package includes 125 graphics ready for use. Package provides sample of other Print Shop libraries, including holidays, animals, etc. Also included are twelve fonts.

Name: **Print Shop Deluxe Sampler Graphics Collection for Windows**

Program type: Clip art

Vendor: Broderbund Software, Inc.

Cost: $44.95
Hardware requirements: IBM compatible; 1MB disk space
Additional software needed: Print Shop Deluxe; Windows 3.x
Description: The package includes 125 graphics ready for use. Package provides sample of other Print Shop libraries, including holidays, animals, etc. Also included are twelve fonts.

Name: **Print Shop Graphics for Libraries: Volume 1**
Program type: Clip art
Vendor: Libraries Unlimited
Cost: $25 (Apple); $25.50 (IBM)
Hardware requirements: Apple; IBM compatible
Additional software needed: Print Shop or New Print Shop (not all graphics can be used with New Print Shop), Print Shop Companion (original)
Description: This is the original, 1989 version of graphics specifically geared to library needs for use with the Print Shop. This first volume contains library-theme material suitable for bookmarks, library signs, etc.

Name: **Print Shop Graphics for Libraries: Volume 2: Perpetual Calendars**
Program type: Clip art
Vendor: Libraries Unlimited
Cost: $24 (Apple); $24.50 (IBM)
Hardware requirements: Apple; IBM compatible
Additional software needed: Print Shop
Description: Need some calendars? This is the one that will combine with your Print Shop to print a variety of calendars for any month or year. (New Print Shop will not work with this set.)

Name: **Print Shop Graphics for Libraries: Volume 3: Books and Fonts**
Program type: Clip art
Vendor: Libraries Unlimited
Cost: $23.50 (Apple); $23.75 (IBM)
Hardware requirements: Apple; IBM compatible
Additional software needed: Print Shop or New Print Shop.
Description: More than 100 graphics show people in various settings to promote reading. The program also contains 15 decorative and happy fonts.

Name: **Print Shop Graphics for Libraries: Volume 4: Dynamic Library Graphics**

Program type: Clip art

Vendor: Libraries Unlimited

Cost: $26 (Apple); $27 (IBM); $26.75 (Macintosh)

Hardware requirements: Apple; IBM compatible; Macintosh

Additional software needed: Print Shop or New Print Shop (Macintosh version requires Print Shop Mac)

Description: This may be the most useful disk for libraries. It contains people of all ages and types reading in many situations. It also shows books and literary characters, etc.

Name: **Print Shop Graphics for Libraries: Volume 5: States and Politics**

Program type: Clip art

Vendor: Libraries Unlimited

Cost: $26.50 (Apple); $27.25 (IBM)

Hardware requirements: Apple; IBM compatible

Additional software needed: Print Shop or New Print Shop (not all graphics can be used with New Print Shop)

Description: The program contains both 100 graphics and 14 high resolution screen displays of maps of states, regions, flags, monuments, political and patriotic symbols, etc.

Name: **Print Shop Graphics for Libraries: Volume 6: American Heritage**

Program type: Clip art

Vendor: Libraries Unlimited

Cost: $27.50

Hardware requirements: Apple; IBM compatible

Additional software needed: Print Shop or New Print Shop (not all graphics can be used with New Print Shop)

Description: This selection of images provides useful material about the frontier days, WWI and WWII, Vietnam, etc.

Name: **Print Shop Graphics for Libraries: Volume 7: World Nations and History**

Program type: Clip art

Vendor: Libraries Unlimited

Cost: $28 (Apple); $28.50 (IBM)

Hardware requirements: Apple; IBM compatible

Additional software needed: Print Shop or New Print Shop (not all graphics can be used with New Print Shop)

Description: This exciting selection of world historical figures (e.g., Hitler, King Tut, Napoleon) provides a useful addition to clip art collection for use with flyers, newsletters, etc.

Name: **Print Shop Graphics for Libraries: Volume 8**
Program type: Clip art
Vendor: Libraries Unlimited
Cost: $22.75 (Apple); $23.75 (IBM)
Hardware requirements: Apple; IBM compatible
Additional software needed: Print Shop or New Print Shop
Description: This set contains many symbols familiar to librarians. The international symbol of libraries, and its many permutations, can be used for local library flavor.

Name: **Print Shop Graphics for Libraries: Volume 9: Computers and Audiovisual**
Program type: Clip art
Vendor: Libraries Unlimited
Cost: $26.75
Hardware requirements: Macintosh
Additional software needed: Print Shop Mac
Description: The set contains more than 100 graphics suitable for use with children's programs, announcement flyers, posters, and newsletters. Featured are cartoon animals, computer pirates, etc., all engaged in AV or computer use. The graphics can be used with any program that will accept MacPaint files.

Name: **Print Shop Graphics Library: School & Business Edition**
Program type: Clip art
Vendor: Broderbund Software, Inc.
Cost: $34.95
Hardware requirements: IBM compatible; 1MB disk space
Additional software needed: New Print Shop
Description: The program contains many clip art selections that can be used with New Print Shop or a compatible program. Scenes depict people in educational and business settings.

Name: **Publique Art: Public Domain Clip Art**
Program type: Clip art on CD-ROM
Vendor: Quanta Press, Inc.

Cost: $99.95
Hardware requirements: IBM compatible; CD-ROM drive
Additional software needed: Any program that uses PCX format
Description: This collection of more than 2,500 public domain graphics is in PCX format.

Name: **School PCX Pictures**
Program type: Clip art
Vendor: Software Labs
Cost: $3.69; $4.69 for 3.5-inch format
Hardware requirements: IBM compatible
Additional software needed: Any software package that accepts PCX files
Description: The program is useful for school librarians who need images for flyers, brochures, and newsletters representing the school environment. It contains images of students working at their desks studying, schools, teachers, computer classes, and graduation.

Name: **Symbols & Slogans**
Program type: Clip art
Vendor: TimeWorks, Inc.
Cost: $39.95
Hardware requirements: IBM compatible
Additional software needed: Publish It!
Description: The program contains 450 signs and symbols of many types for many uses.

Name: **Vielhaber Clip Art for PFS First Publisher**
Program type: Clip art
Vendor: Software Labs
Cost: $3.69 (shareware)
Hardware requirements: IBM compatible
Additional software needed: PFS First Publisher
Description: This is an excellent set of clip art images, many suitable for library newsletters and flyers. Images depict signs, autos, flowers, animals, people, and even a bookshelf or two.

Name: **WetPaint**
Program type: Clip art
Vendor: DUBL-Click
Cost: $79.95 each (10 volumes)
Hardware requirements: Macintosh; 128KB RAM minimum

Additional software needed: Microsoft Word, ArtRoundup

Description: WetPaint's ten different collections of clip art contain much variety: borders, symbols, animals, people, etc. Each collection contains clip art tools such as erase, pencil, slideshow, etc., and ways of rotating, flipping, inverting, bit shifting, mirroring, and generating random patterns. ArtRoundup desk accessory opens and displays the paint files. Volume 19/20 includes 12- and 24-point fonts: Alexandra, Aswan, etc. Also contains Hieroglyphics font, Egyptian borders, etc.

Name: **WordPerfect Art**

Program type: Clip art

Vendor: Reasonable Solutions

Cost: $4 each (5 volumes) (shareware)

Hardware requirements: IBM compatible

Additional software needed: WordPerfect 5.0, 5.1, or WordPerfect for Windows

Description: Each shareware disk contains more than 90 selected pieces of clip art.

Name: **Works of Art Laser Art Business Selection**

Program type: Clip art

Vendor: Spinnaker Software Corp.

Cost: $99.95

Hardware requirements: Macintosh; IBM compatible

Additional software needed: Any program that uses PostScript clip art

Description: The package contains 125 EPS illustrations: Americana, arts, business, celebrations, computers, dingbats and symbols, landscapes and scenery, maps, travel, etc.

Name: **Works of Art Samplers**

Program type: Clip art

Vendor: Spinnaker Software Corp.

Cost: $39.95 each (3 samplers)

Hardware requirements: Macintosh

Additional software needed: Any program that uses PostScript clip art

Description: Each of three products—Education Series Sampler, Holiday Series Sampler, HyperCard Stackware—contains more than 500 EPS illustrations.

Scanning Software

In addition to using fully prepared clip art, computer graphic images can be created by scanning photographs and other documents. Scanning will digitize a document in basically the same way that a fax does. Once a photo or document has been scanned by either a full-page scanner or a hand-held scanner, the computer can further edit it. Most of the software that follows is for scanning text. If text is being scanned, a special optical character recognition software package must be used to interpret it correctly.

Name:	**CatchWord 1.2**
Program type:	Optical character recognition
Vendor:	Logitech, Inc.
Cost:	$249
Hardware requirements:	IBM compatible; ScanMan scanner; 640KB RAM minimum; 1MB disk space
Description:	Catchword transforms ScanMan text into ASCII format. Its built-in font recognition technology makes training unnecessary. The program will work with text scanned horizontally or vertically, in columns or full page. Text can be imported from other scanners as well. It will recognize 6- to 20-point characters in 11 languages. Material can be typeset, typewritten, kerned, near-letter-quality dot matrix, bold, italic, or underlined. Graphics are removed automatically from text. The program uses pull-down menus.

Name:	**CatchWord Pro for Macintosh**
Program type:	Optical character recognition
Vendor:	Logitech, Inc.
Cost:	$399
Hardware requirements:	Macintosh; 2MB RAM minimum; ScanMan Model 32
Description:	The program is similar to Catchword, but it is for the Macintosh. Processed text is saved in a variety of for-

mats, including ASCII text, WordPerfect, Word, among others, in English, French, or German.

Name:	**CatchWord Pro for Windows 1.0**
Program type:	Optical character recognition
Vendor:	Logitech, Inc.
Cost:	$299
Hardware requirements:	IBM compatible; 4MB RAM minimum; 3MB disk space; ScanMan scanner
Additional software needed:	Windows 3.x
Description:	The program is similar to CatchWord, but it is for the Windows environment. It translates scanned text to 21 different formats, while deleting graphics. Special text features such as italic and column format are kept intact. Text in 11 languages can be scanned.

Name:	**OmniPage 3.0**
Program type:	Optical character recognition
Vendor:	Caere Corp.
Cost:	$695
Hardware requirements:	Macintosh; 5MB RAM minimum; 4MB disk space; HP ScanJet IIc scanner
Description:	This program will scan virtually any text in any font or size or column format and convert it to word processor, spreadsheet, or database requirements. It also works with graphics. The package is particularly noted for its speed. It recognizes nonstylized fonts from 6 to 72 points. Text is displayed in Transient Editor to allow the user to check for correctness and to make necessary changes. Thirty file formats are supported.

Name:	**OmniPage Professional 2.0**
Program type:	Optical character recognition
Vendor:	Caere Corp.
Cost:	$995
Hardware requirements:	Macintosh; 5MB RAM minimum; 4MB disk space; HP ScanJet IIc scanner
Description:	This program will scan virtually any text in any font or size or column format and convert it to word processor, spreadsheet, or database requirements. It also works with graphics. The package is particularly noted for its speed. It recognizes nonstylized fonts from 6 to 72 points. Text is displayed in Transient Editor to allow the user to check

for correctness and to make necessary changes. Thirty file formats are supported. The program has more power than OmniPage, preceding, plus custom characters, graphics editor, and much more.

Name:	**OmniPage Professional for Windows 2.0**
Program type:	Optical character recognition
Vendor:	Caere Corp.
Cost:	$995
Hardware requirements:	IBM compatible; 4MB RAM minimum; 8MB disk space; HP ScanJet IIc scanner
Additional software needed:	Windows 3.x
Description:	This program will scan virtually any text in any font or size or column format and convert it to word processor, spreadsheet, or database requirements. It also works with graphics. The package is particularly noted for its speed. It recognizes nonstylized fonts from 6 to 72 points. Text is displayed in Transient Editor to allow the user to check for correctness and to make necessary changes. Thirty file formats are supported. The program has more power than OmniPage, preceding, plus custom characters, graphics editor, and much more.

Name:	**Perceive Personal 2.0**
Program type:	Optical character recognition
Vendor:	OCRON, Inc.
Cost:	$195
Hardware requirements:	IBM compatible; 2MB RAM minimum; 4MB disk space
Description:	For use with handheld scanners, Perceive Personal will recognize underlined, bold, italic, and proportionally spaced characters and even dot matrix print. The merge feature will combine separate sections of scanned text into the original single sheet. Text from 8 to 36 points is recognized. The program includes capability for eleven European languages and works at 300 dpi.

Name:	**WordScan 1.1**
Program type:	Optical character recognition
Vendor:	Calera Recognition Systems
Cost:	$295
Hardware requirements:	Macintosh; 2MB RAM minimum; 6MB disk space
Description:	This character recognition program performs optical character recognition from 6 to 28 points for word pro-

cessing, desktop publishing, and many other applications. Formatting is retained. As it reads a scanned document, it will automatically save text to one file and each graphics image to a separate file.

Name:	**WordScan for Windows 1.1**
Program type:	Optical character recognition
Vendor:	Calera Recognition Systems
Cost:	$595
Hardware requirements:	IBM compatible; 2MB RAM minimum; 6MB disk space
Additional software needed:	Windows 3.x
Description:	This character recognition program performs optical character recognition from 6 to 28 points for word processing, desktop publishing, and many other applications. Formatting is retained. As it reads a scanned document, it will automatically save text to one file and each graphics image to a separate file.

Name:	**WordScan Plus 1.1**
Program type:	Optical character recognition
Vendor:	Calera Recognition Systems
Cost:	$595 (Macintosh); $995 (DOS)
Hardware requirements:	IBM compatible or Macintosh; 2MB RAM minimum; 6MB disk space
Description:	Additional features in this program that go beyond those offered in the original WordScan, preceding, include on-screen viewing of scanned images and the designated page areas to be scanned, and special fax operation. Style sheets offer greater flexibility in the processing of data that has been scanned.

Name:	**WordScan Plus for Windows 1.1**
Program type:	Optical character recognition
Vendor:	Calera Recognition Systems
Cost:	$995
Hardware requirements:	IBM compatible; 2MB RAM minimum; 6MB disk space
Additional software needed:	Windows 3.x
Description:	Additional features in this program that go beyond those offered in the original WordScan, preceding, include on-screen viewing of scanned images and the designated page areas to be scanned, and special fax operation. Style sheets offer greater flexibility in the processing of data that has been scanned.

Vendor List

Activision, Inc.
11440 San Vicente Blvd., Suite 3000
Los Angeles, CA 94039
(800) 477-3650; (310) 207-4500

Adobe Systems, Inc.
1585 Charleston Rd.
P.O. Box 7900
Mountain View, CA 94043
(800) 833-6687

Advanced Software, Inc.
1095 E. Duane Ave., #103
Sunnyvale, CA 94086
(800) 346-5392; (408) 733-0745

Aldus Corp.
411 1st Ave. S., Suite 200
Seattle, WA 98104
(800) 685-3540; (206) 622-5500

Altsys Corp.
269 W. Renner Rd.
Richardson, TX 75080
(214) 680-2060

American Training International
12638 Beatrice St.
Los Angeles, CA 90066
(310) 823-1129

Applied Microsystems
200 W. 34th Ave., #571
Anchorage, AK 99503
(800) 327-2588

Ares Software Corp.
561 Pilgrim Dr., Suite D
Foster City, CA 94404
(415) 578-9090

Artbeats
2611 S. Myrtle Rd., Box 1287
(800) 444-9392; (503) 863-4429

Artware Systems, Inc.
6512 Six Forks Rd.
Raleigh, NC 27615
(800) 426-3858; (919) 790-7722

Ashton-Tate Corp.
20101 Hamilton Ave.
Torrence, CA 90502
(213) 329-8000

Banner Blue Software, Inc.
39500 Stevenson Pl., Suite 204
Fremont, CA 94539
(510) 794-6850

Baudville Computer Products
5380 52nd St.
Grand Rapids, MI 49512
(800) 728-0888; (616) 698-0888

Beagle Brothers Micro Software, Inc.
6215 Ferris Sq., Suite 100
San Diego, CA 92121
(619) 452-5500

Bitstream, Inc.
215 First St.
Cambridge, MA 02142
(800) 522-3668; (617) 497-6222

Black Orchid Software, Inc.
P.O. Box 58098
St. Petersburg, FL 33715
(800) 277-1379

BLOCPublishing Corp.
800 SW 37th Ave., Suite 765
Coral Gables, FL 33134
(800) 955-1888; (305) 445-0903

Broderbund Software, Inc.
500 Redwood Blvd.
Novato, CA 94948
(800) 521-6263

Brown Wagh Publishing
160 Knowles Dr.
Los Gatos, CA 95030
(800) 451-0900; (408) 378-3838

Caere Corp.
100 Cooper Ct.
Los Gatos, CA 95030
(800) 535-7226; (408) 720-0999

Calera Recognition Systems
2500 Augustine Dr.
Santa Clara, CA 95054
(800) 544-7051

Cassady & Greene, Inc.
P.O. Box 223779
Carmel, CA 93922
(800) 351-0500

Claris Corp.
5201 Patrick Henry Dr.
Santa Clara, CA 95052
(408) 727-8227

ColorAge, Inc.
900 Technology Park Dr.
Billerica, MA 01821
(800) 437-3336; (508) 667-8585

Compugraphic
200 Ballardvale St.
Wilmington, MA 01887
(800) 451-4000; (508) 658-5600

Computer Associates International, Inc.
1 Computer Associates Plaza
Islandia, NY 11788
(800) 225-5224; (516) 342-5224

Computer Showroom
22272 N. Pepper Rd.
Barrington, IL 60010
(708) 382-5108

Computer Support Corp.
15926 Midway Rd.
Dallas, TX 75244
(214) 661-8960

Corel Systems Corp.
1600 Carling Ave., Suite 190
Ottawa, ON K1Z 8R7 Canada
(800) 836-7274; (613) 728-8200

CSI Publishing
13721A Rosewell Ave.
Chino Hills, CA 91710
(916) 756-4158

Custom Applications
900 Technology Park Dr., Bldg. B
Billerica, MA 01821
(508) 667-8585

DataViz, Inc.
55 Corporate Dr.
Trumbull, CT 06611
(800) 733-0030; (203) 268-0030

Delrina Technology, Inc.
6830 Via Del Oro, Suite 240
San Jose, CA 95116
(800) 268-6082; (408) 363-2345

DeltaPoint, Inc.
2 Harris Ct., Suite B-1
Monterey, CA 93940
(800) 446-6955; (408) 648-4000

Deneba Systems
7400 SW 87th Ave.
Miami, FL 33173
(800) 622-6827; (305) 596-5644

Digi-Fonts, Inc.
528 Commons Dr.
Golden, CO 80401
(303) 526-9435

Digital Research, Inc.
70 Garden Ct., P.O. Box DRI
Monterey, CA 93942
(800) 443-4200

Walt Disney Computer Software, Inc.
500 S. Buena Vista St.
Burbank, CA 91521
(800) 688-1520; (818) 973-4015

Dream Maker Software
925 W. Kenyon Ave., Suite 16
Englewood, CO 80110
(800) 876-5665; (303) 762-1001

DUBL-Click Software
22521 Styles St.
Woodland Hills, CA 91367
(800) 266-9525; (818) 888-2068

Dynamic Graphics, Inc.
1015 Atlantic Ave.
Peoria, IL 61614
(800) 255-8800

Eastern Digital Resources
P.O. Box 1451
Clearwater, SC 29822
(803) 593-0870

Educorp.
7434 Trade St.
San Diego, CA 92121
(800) 843-9497; (619) 536-9999

Electronic Arts
1450 Fashion Island Blvd.
San Mateo, CA 94404
(800) 245-4525; (415) 571-7171

Emerald City Software
P.O. Box 2103
Menlo Park, CA 94026

Enabling Technologies Co.
3102 S.E. Jay St.
Stuart, FL 34997
(407) 283-4817

Epyx, Inc.
500 Allerton St.
Redwood City, CA 94063
(415) 368-3200

Expert Software
800 Douglas Entrance, North Tower,
Suite 355
Coral Gables, FL 33134
(800) 759-2562; (305) 567-9990

Expressware
Box 1800
Duvall, WA 98019
(800) 753-3453; (206) 788-0932

FGM, Inc.
131 Elden St., Suite 308
Herndon, VA 22070
(800) 783-7428; (703) 478-9881

Frame Technology Corp.
1010 Rincon Circle
San Jose, CA 95131
(800) 843-7263; (408) 433-3311

Funk Software, Inc.
222 Third St.
Cambridge, MA 02142
(800) 822-3865, ext. 212; (617) 497-6339

GeoWorks, Inc.
2150 Shattuck Ave.
Berkeley, CA 94704
(800) 772-0001; (415) 644-0883

Halcyon Software
1590 La Pradera
Campbell, CA 95014
(408) 378-9898

Haven Tree Software Ltd.
P.O. Box 1083-P
Thousand Island Park, NY 13692
(800) 267-0668; (613) 544-6035

Hi Tech Expressions
584 Broadway
New York, NY 10012
(212) 941-1521

HSC Software
1661 Lincoln Blvd., Suite 101
Santa Monica, CA 90404
(310) 392-8441

Imageline, Inc.
6502 Dickens Place
Richmond, VA 23219
(800) 368-3773; (804) 673-5601

ISS International Software Systems, Inc.
202 6th SW, Suite 650
Calgary, AL T2P 2R9 Canada
(403) 233-2520

Lasertools Corp.
1250 45th St., Suite 100
Emeryville, CA 94608
(800) 767-8004; (510) 420-8777

The Learning Company
6493 Kaiser Dr.
Fremont, CA 94555
(800) 852-2255

LEI, Inc.
RR1, P.O. Box 219
New Albany, PA 18833
(717) 746-1842; FAX: 717-746-1114

LetraSet USA
40 Eisenhower Dr.
Paramus, NJ 07653
(800) 343-8973; (201) 845-6100

Libraries Unlimited, Inc.
P.O. Box 3988
Englewood, CO 80155
(303) 770-1220

Logitech, Inc.
6505 Kaiser Dr.
Fremont, CA 94555
(800) 231-7717; (510) 495-8500

Lotus Development Corp.
55 Cambridge Pkwy.
Cambridge, MA 02142
(800) 343-5414; (617) 577-8500

MacAcademy
477 S. Nova Rd.
Ormond Beach, FL 32174
(904) 677-1918

McCarthy-McCormick, Inc.
1440 Oak Hills Dr.
Colorado Springs, CO 80919

Mainstay
5311-B Derry Ave.
Agoura Hills, CA 91301
(818) 991-6540

Managing Editor Software, Inc.
101 Greenwood Ave.
Jenkintown Plaza, Suite 160
Jenkintown, PA 19046
(800) 638-1214; (215) 886-5662

Manhattan Graphics Corp.
250 E. Hartsdale Ave.
Hartsdale, NY 10530
(800) 572-6533; (914) 725-2048

Mastersoft, Inc.
6991 E. Camelback Rd., Suite A320
Scottsdale, AZ 85251
(800) 624-6107; (602) 277-0900

Melody Hall
See Computer Showroom

Micrografx
1303 Arapaho
Richardson, TX 75081
(800) 733-3729; (214) 234-1769

Microsoft Corp.
1 Microsoft Way
Redmond, WA 98052
(800) 426-9400; (206) 882-8080

Micromap Map
9642 W. Virginia Circle
Lakewood, CO 80226
(303) 988-4940

MicroVideo Learning Systems
91 Fifth Ave., 6th Fl.
New York, NY 10003
(800) 231-4021; (212) 255-0053

Mindplay
Box 36491
Tucson, AZ 85740
(800) 221-7911

Mindscape
3444 Dundee Rd.
Northbrook, IL 60062
(800) 221-9884; (708) 480-7668

Mouse Systems Corp.
47505 Seabridge Dr.
Fremont, CA 94538
(510) 656-1117

NewDEST Corp.
1015 E. Brokaw Rd.
San Jose, CA 95131
(800) 822-8884; (408) 436-2700

OCRON, Inc.
3350 Scott Blvd., Bldg. 36
Santa Clara, CA 95054
(800) 933-1399; (408) 980-8900

Personal Training Systems
828 S. Bascom Ave., Suite 100
San Jose, CA 95128
(800) 832-2499; (408) 286-1635

S. H. Pierce & Co.
1 Kendall Sq., Suite 323, Bldg. 600
Cambridge, MA 02139
(617) 395-8350

Pinnacle Publishing Inc.
P.O. Box 888
Kent, WA 98035
(800) 788-1900; (206) 251-1900

Portfolio Systems, Inc.
10062 Miller Ave., Suite 201
Cupertino, CA 95041
(800) 729-3866; (408) 252-0420

Postcraft International, Inc.
27811 Avenue Hopkins, Suite 6
Valencia, CA 91355
(805) 257-1797

Power Up! Software Corp.
2929 Campus Dr.
San Mateo, CA 94403
(800) 851-2917; (415) 345-5900

Public Domain Exchange
2074C Walsh Ave., Dept. 707
Santa Clara, CA 95050
(800) 331-8125; (408) 496-0624

Quanta Press, Inc.
1313 Fifth St. SE, Suite 208C
Minneapolis, MN 55414
(612) 379-3956

Quark, Inc.
1800 Grant
Denver, CO 80203
(800) 788-7835; (303) 894-8888

Que Software
11711 N. College Ave.
Carmel, IN 46032
(800) 992-0244; (317) 573-2583

Reasonable Solutions
2101 W. Main St.
Medford, OR 97501
(800) 503-3475

Reference Software International
330 Townsend St., Suite 119
San Francisco, CA 94107
(415) 541-0509

Samna Corp.
5600 Glenridge Dr.
Atlanta, GA 30342
(404) 851-0007

Scholastic, Inc.
2931 E. McCarty St.
Jefferson City, MO 65102
(800) 541-5513

Sensible Software
20200 E. 9 Mile Rd., Suite 150
St. Clair, MI 48080
(800) 394-4669; (313) 774-7215

Serif
P.O. Box 803
Nashua, NH 03061
(800) 869-8909; (603) 889-8650

Silicon Beach Software
9770 Carroll Center Rd., Suite J
San Diego, CA 92126
(619) 695-6956

SkiSoft Publishing Corp.
1644 Massachusetts Ave., Suite 79
Lexington, MA 02173
(800) 662-3622; (617) 863-1876

SoftCraft, Inc.
16 N. Carroll, Suite 500
Madison, WI 53703
(800) 351-0500; (608) 257-3300

Softsync
800 Douglas Entrance, North Tower
Coral Gables, FL 33134
(305) 444-0080

Software Labs
3767 Overland Ave., #112
Los Angeles, CA 90034
(310) 559-5456

Software Publishing Corporation
3165 Kifer Rd.
Santa Clara, CA 95051
(408) 986-8000

Solutions Unlimited
Box 12053
Overland Park, KS 66212
(913) 451-0110

Spinnaker Software Corp.
201 Broadway
Cambridge, MA 02139
(800) 323-8088; (617) 494-1219

StatSoft
2325 E. 13th St.
Tulsa, OK 74104
(918) 583-4149

Studio Advertising Art
P.O. Box 43915
Las Vegas, NV 89116
(702) 641-7041

**Sunburst Communications, Inc.
(Wings for Learning)**
1600 Green Hills Rd.
P.O. Box 660002
Scotts Valley, CA 95067
(800) 321-7511

SuperMac Technology, Inc.
485 Potero Ave.
Sunnyvale, CA 94086
(800) 335-3005; (408) 245-2202

SWFTE International, Ltd.
P.O. Box 219
Rockland, DE 19732
(800) 237-9383; (302) 234-1740

Symantec Corp.
10201 Torre Ave.
Cupertino, CA 95014
(800) 441-7234; (408) 253-9600

Target Software, Inc.
P.O. Box 1687
Allentown, PA 18105
(215) 820-9394

TerraVision, Inc.
2351 College Station Rd., Suite 563
Athens, GA 30605
(800) TGL-PLUS; (706) 769-5641

3-D Graphics Corp.
11410 NE 124th St., #6155
Kirkland, WA 98034
(800) 456-0234

TimeWorks, Inc.
625 Academy Dr.
Northbrook, IL 60062
(800) 323-7744; (708) 559-1300

T/Maker Company
1390 Villa St.
Mountain View, CA 94041
(415) 962-0195

Unison World Software
1321 Harbor Bay Pkwy.
Alameda, CA 94501
(800) 444-7553; (510) 748-6670

Ventura Software
15175 Innovation Dr.
San Diego, CA 92128
(800) 822-8221; (619) 673-0172

Video and Image Compression Corp.
2221 Rosecrans Ave.
El Segundo, CA 90245
(800) 472-1888; (310) 643-7571

Video Professor
Available through Library Video Company
P.O. Box 1110
Bala Cynwyd, PA 19004
(800) 843-3620; (215) 667-0200

Roger Wagner Publishing
1050 Pioneer Way, Suite P
El Cajon, CA 92020
(619) 442-0522

Wayzata Technology, Inc.
P.O. Box 807
Grand Rapids, MN 55744
(800) 735-7321; (218) 326-0597

WordPerfect Corporation
1555 N. Technology Way
Orem, UT 84057
(800) 451-5151; (801) 225-5000

WordStar International, Inc.
201 Alameda Del Prado
Novato, CA 94949
(800) 227-5609; (415) 382-8000

Zedcor, Inc.
4500 E. Speedway Blvd., Suite 22
Tucson, AZ 85712
(800) 482-4567; (602) 881-8108

Zenographics
4 Executive Circle, Suite 200
Irvine, CA 92714
(800) 366-7494; (714) 851-6352

ZSoft Corp.
450 Franklin Rd., #100
Marietta, GA 30067
(800) 444-4780; (404) 428-0008

Suggested Reading

Desktop Publishing—Applications Manuals

Schenck, Mary, and Randi Benton. *The Official New Print Shop Handbook*. New York: Bantam, 1990.

Desktop Publishing—General

Crawford, Walt. *Desktop Publishing for Librarians*. Boston: G.K. Hall, 1990.
Johnson, Richard D., and Harriett H. Johnson. *The Macintosh Press: Desktop Publishing for Libraries*. Westport, Conn.: Meckler, 1989.
Kruse, Benedict. *Desktop Publishing: Producing Professional Publications*. Albany, N.Y.: Delmar Publishers, Inc., 1989.
Lamar, Laura. *Desktop Design*. Los Altos, Calif.: Crisp Publications, 1990.
Manousos, Stephen, and Scott Tilden. *The Professional Look: The Complete Guide to Desktop Publishing*. San Jose, Calif.: Venture Perspectives Press, 1991.
Schaeffer, Mark. *Library Displays Handbook*. New York: Wilson, 1991.
Schenck, Mary, and Randi Benton. *The Official New Print Shop Handbook*. New York: Bantam, 1990.
Tufte, Edward R. *The Visual Display of Quantitative Information*. Cheshire, Conn.: Graphics Press, 1987.
Weiner, Ed. *Desktop Publishing Made Simple*. New York: Doubleday, 1991.

Dictionaries

Que's Computer User's Dictionary. Carmel, Ind.: Que Corp., 1991.

Electronic Mail

Dewey, Patrick R. *Email for Libraries*. Westport, Conn.: Meckler, 1990.

DOS

Gookin, Dan. *DOS Secrets: An Easy Guide to Understanding the Power of MS-DOS*. San Diego, Calif.: Computer Publishing Enterprises, 1990.

FAX

Dewey, Patrick R. *FAX for Libraries*. Westport, Conn.: Meckler, 1990.

Handbooks

Costa, Betty and Marie. *A Micro Handbook for Small Libraries and Media Centers*, 3d ed. Englewood, Colo.: Libraries Unlimited, 1991.

Hardware

Cummings, Steve, et al. *LaserJet IIP Essentials*. Emeryville, Calif.: Peachpit Press, 1990.
Pfeiffer, Katherine Shelly. *The LaserJet Font Book*. Emeryville, Calif.: Peachpit Press, 1990.
Pina, Larry. *Macintosh Printer Secrets*. Carmel, Ind.: Hayden, 1990.
Polly, Jean Armour, et al. *Essential Guide to Apple Computers in Libraries: Hardware Set-Up and Expansion*. Westport, Conn.: Meckler, 1987.
Salkind, Neil J. *The Big Mac Book*. Carmel, Ind.: Que Corp., 1989.
Sheldon, Thomas. *Hard Disk Management in the PC & MS DOS Environment*. New York: McGraw-Hill, 1988.

Layout and Design

Parker, Roger C. *The Makeover Book: 101 Design Solutions for Desktop Publishing*. Chapel Hill, N.C.: Ventana Press, 1989.
Williams, Robin. *Five Steps to a Better Layout: Basic Design Principles for Desktop Publishers*. Santa Rosa, Calif.: PEP, 1989.

Local Area Networks

Desmarais, Norman, ed. *CD-ROM Local Area Networks: A User's Guide*. Westport, Conn.: Meckler, 1990.

Marks, Kenneth, and Steven Nielsen. *Local Area Networks in Libraries*. Westport, Conn.: Meckler, 1991.

Understanding Computer Networks. Westport, Conn.: Addison-Wesley, 1989.

Wright, Keith. *Workstations and Local Area Networks for Librarians*. Chicago: American Library Association, 1990.

Projects and Project Management

Dewey, Patrick R. *101 Microcomputer Projects to Do in Your Library*. Chicago: American Library Association, 1990.

Lane, Elizabeth. *Microcomputer Management and Maintenance for Libraries*. Westport, Conn.: Meckler, 1990.

Public Access

Dewey, Patrick R. *Public Access Microcomputers: A Handbook for Librarians*, 2d ed. Boston: G.K. Hall, 1990.

Duke, John K., and Arnold Hirshon. "Policies for Microcomputers in Libraries: An Administrative Model." *Information Technology and Libraries* 193 (Sept. 1986).

Polly, Jean Armour. *Essential Guide to Apple Computers in Libraries*. Westport, Conn.: Meckler, 1986.

Reference

Dewey, Patrick R. *Microcomputers and the Reference Librarian*. Westport, Conn.: Meckler, 1989.

Software

Cargill, Jennifer, ed. *Integrated Online Library Catalogs*. Westport, Conn.: Meckler, 1990.

Dewey, Patrick R. *Interactive Fiction and Adventure Games*, 2d ed. Westport, Conn.: Meckler, 1991.

Glossbrenner, Alfred. *Alfred Glossbrenner's Master Guide to Free Software for IBMs and Compatible Computers*. New York: St. Martin's Press, 1989.

Lawrence, Anthony. *Software, Copyright, and Competition: The "Look and Feel" of the Law*. Westport, Conn.: Quorum Books, 1989.

Mace, Paul. *The Paul Mace Guide to Data Recovery*. New York: Simon & Schuster, 1988.

Machalow, Robert. *Using Microsoft Excel*. New York: Neal-Schuman, 1991.

Software Cataloging

Holzberlein, Deanne. *Computer Software Cataloging: Techniques and Examples*. New York: Haworth Press, 1986.

Software Directories

Bowker. *The Software Encyclopedia*. New Providence, N.J.: R.R. Bowker, 1992.

Buckleitner, Warren. *Survey of Early Childhood Software*. Ypsilanti, Mich.: High/Scope Press, 1989.

Dewey, Patrick R. *202+ Software Packages to Use in Your Library* (101 Micro Series). Chicago: American Library Association, 1992.

Dlug, Paul. *Microsoft Works 2.0: IBM Applications*. Blue Ridge Summit, Pa.: Windcrest Books, 1990.

Macintosh Product Registry. Quarterly. Vero Beach, Fl.: Redgate Communications Corp. Subscription. $40/yr.

Word Processing

LaPier, Cynthia B. *The Librarian's Guide to WordPerfect 5.0*. Westport, Conn.: Meckler, 1990.

McClure, Rhyder, and Steven Cherry. *Desktop Publishing with WordPerfect 5.0 and 5.1*. New York: Brady, 1990.

Glossary

Accelerator board   A circuit card that is added to the main (mother) board of a computer to speed up the machine and increase performance. Some work for graphics, some for math (math co-processors), and some speed up the general performance, such as Intel's Overdrive Processor.

Arched or arching   A special effect whereby a line of text or headline is bent to form an arch.

ASCII   *A*merican *S*tandard *C*ode for *I*nformation *I*nterchange is an agreed upon standard of 128 letters, numbers, and other symbols. Each symbol is represented by a set of seven digits (*1*s and *0*s).

Backup   A second or additional copy on a disk of a program or data.

Batch   Multiple instructions or data executed as a group, often as if typed from the keyboard (especially when used as a macro).

Baud   Bits per second transmitted. Typically, data speed is 300 baud (300 bits per second), 1200, 2400, 9600, etc. Since each computer character requires about ten bits (including stop, start, etc., bits), this amounts to 30, 120, 240, etc., characters per second.

Bezier curve   A curve generated by a mathematical formula as opposed to a bitmapped curve.

Bit   The smallest unit of information that a computer can process, either a *1* or a *0*. Bits are combined into groups of eight or more to form a byte.

Bitmap   A literal representation of an image in computer memory. Each bit (or several bits in the case of color images) represents one pixel (picture element). The opposite of bitmap is EPS (Encapsulated PostScript) in which images are represented (or described) by mathematical formulas.

Blend   A special tool for blending computer images from color to color. Blending tools are useful for increasing the realistic look of a picture.

BMP   Bitmap graphics format for Windows applications.

Body type   Usually 10-point type that is used for the body (paragraph) text of a document.

Boot   The process of starting up a computer to prepare it for service. Usually, a small "bootstrap" program is loaded in automatically, making it possible to then load other programs. A cold boot is performed when the power to the unit is first turned on, a warm boot when the machine is already on but needs to be reset for some reason.

BSAVE   A binary file format used in some programs.

Bullet text   Special marks, such as dots or boxes, that are used to highlight a series of items on separate lines after an initial explanation. Boxes are usually used in check-off order forms.

Bulletin board system   An interactive online database that may have a number of features, including multiple lines in, upload/download of public domain and shareware programs, electronic mail, conference areas, etc. Usually, though not always, it is operated on a local microcomputer. Some operate on national networks such as the Source or CompuServe.

Byte   Generally, 8 bits used during transmission, though stop and start bits may make it 10 bits. A byte is basically a computer word (character) such as *W* or *1*.

CD-ROM   *C*ompact *D*isk–*R*ead-*O*nly *M*emory is a recently introduced storage device that differs in several important ways from conventional disk drives. It will hold several hundred megabytes of data and is more difficult to damage. A major problem with CD-ROM is that data on it cannot be erased. The WORM (*W*rite *O*nce–*R*ead *M*any) is an effort to overcome this deficiency.

Central processing unit (CPU)   The central brain or processor of the computer where timing, routing of data, and other decisions are made.

Character set   A full set of the numbers, letters, and other characters used by a computer. A typical character set is extended ASCII code with 256 characters.

Chip   The basic hardware unit of microcomputer technology, made of silicon.

Circuit board   A board that contains a number of chips and controls a device, such as a printer or modem, or houses the RAM and ROM (memory) of the computer.

Click art   Another name for clip art that is in electronic format.

Clip art   Artwork available from many sources that can be loaded into a desktop publishing or graphics package and used to complete a document.

Clone   A computer that emulates a more-popular brand to capitalize upon the market.

Compatibility   The ability of software to migrate successfully from machine to machine. For example, IBM compatible software will not run on Macintosh equipment. There are further issues regarding monitors, printers, and just about every other aspect of computing. Some software packages are incompatible with each other, or may take some tricky custom work to make several packages work together successfully.

Co-processor   A second or additional central processing unit in a computer.

CP/M operating system   *C*ontrol *P*rogram for *M*icroprocessors was one of the first and most popular of the operating systems available for microcomputers. A large body of public domain software contributed to its popularity.

Crash   A total, and usually sudden, system failure.

CRT   *C*athode *R*ay *T*ube, referring to the monitor or TV screen used for computer program display.

Cursor   Usually a flashing square pointing to where the next character on the computer screen will appear.

Dedicated A program, telephone line, or other device used for a single purpose or function.

Default Factory settings, hardware or software, that typically take over when the computer operator fails to make a conscious decision.

Desk accessory A Macintosh-related term meaning that a program is available at all times from the main Apple menu. An application can be user-defined as a desk accessory with the System 7.

Desktop publishing Creating camera-ready copy with the computer and printer, often entailing a laser printer for high-quality production. Also refers to simpler products produced on a dot matrix printer and programs such as the Print Shop.

Dialogue box Computer query for information that calls for a yes/no, proceed, etc., response.

Digital *1*s and *0*s (digits) that are added into bytes to form computer words or characters, as opposed to the analog or continuous signal of the telephone lines.

Dingbats A very interesting and useful character set of symbols that contains stars, circles, numbers, etc., and is sold by International Typeface Corp. Their official name is ITC Zapf Dingbats.

DIP switch *D*ual *I*n-Line *P*ackage or the set of switches on a computer device that permits it to be used with a variety of computers. This flexibility is important because most manufacturers do not know what kind of computer their product will be used with later.

Disk A small circular object on which data is stored and retrieved and used in a disk drive.

Disk drive The mass-storage device that reads and writes on a disk. These data-storage devices come in many sizes and types and may be built in or external to the computer.

Disk operating system (DOS) The master control program that manages the filing system and interfaces with the disk drives.

Display type Type suitable for headlines and titles.

Dithering The simulation of halftones by using black-and-white pixels in cluster arrangements.

Documentation The printed or online manuals that give the instructions for use of a program.

Dots per inch (dpi) A measurement of resolution usually applied to printers and monitors. The greater the dpi, the better the resolution. For most desktop publishing application printing 300 dpi is acceptable.

Download To receive a program into a computer from a (usually) remote or distant computer. Opposite of ''upload.'' The program can then be copied to disk for future use.

Drawing program A software package that uses vector graphics format to design and illustrate pages by manipulating each item on a page individually.

Drop cap A capitalized first letter that occupies more than one line. For instance, a drop cap may drop several lines below the first line to make a more impressive appearance.

Electronic mail Sending messages electronically. May be sent locally through a bulletin board system or nationally through a nationwide network.

Ellipse Special tool available in Adobe Illustrator for creating ellipses and circles.

Encapsulated PostScript (EPS)   A file format of the printer page-description language PostScript. The file will contain an image description.

EPS   *See* Encapsulated PostScript.

EPSF   For *E*ncapsulated *P*ost*S*cript *F*ile format.

Error message   Any message that the computer sends as a signal that something is wrong. Example: "Disk Full."

Explode   A graphics arrangement in which a total, a pie chart for example, is broken into a number of constituent parts. Such a graphic makes it easier to emphasize certain aspects of the represented data.

Fills   Found in a paint program; an area of the screen is selected and changed by selecting various colors from the palette.

Font   A complete set of letters, numerals, and symbols in a particular typeface or style.

Format   To initialize a disk for use by the computer.

GEM   For *G*raphics *E*nvironment *M*anager; operating environment is a Graphical User Interface (GUI).

Generic software   Software created for a wide variety of uses rather than dedicated to one use. Includes word processors, database managers, spreadsheets, etc. Opposite of a program that, for example, creates catalog cards exclusively.

GIF   For *G*raphics *I*nterface *F*ormat; an image-encoding format widely used on CompuServe and bulletin board systems for transmitting images by modem.

Gradient   The use of color-shading techniques to create the illusion of depth.

Graphical User Interface (GUI)   A graphic-oriented system for operating a computer. Instead of file names, a desktop full of icons (file folders) is seen. The computer operator points and clicks with a mouse (hand device) and uses pull-down menus.

Graphics   A broadly used term that describes the management and use of computer images. The term can be used to describe vector graphics (object-oriented) or raster graphics (bitmapped).

Grayscale   Literally, shades of gray in a black-and-white imaging system. The more shades available, the more realistic an image will look.

Greek   The use of nonsense words or even Latin to fill in a page to see how the overall design or display will look without having to provide the text in advance.

Halftone   A photograph that has had its gradations of tone broken into dots. Such a processed photograph will print much better in a newsletter, newspaper, or other paper product.

Hardcopy   Printed computer data.

Hardware   The nuts-and-bolts parts of the computer that can be seen and felt, such as monitor, chips, keyboard, disk drives, etc.

Hertz   Usually Megahertz, a measurement of millions of cycles. The greater the hertz the faster the computer.

Housekeeping   Maintenance programs or activities designed to keep a system up to working specifications.

Hypertext The ability in a database to jump from highlighted word to highlighted word with no intervening search requests required. Often seen in the newer multimedia encyclopedias on CD-ROM.

Icon A graphic representation of an object, such as a file folder, trash can, or bomb, or a graphic representation of a command.

IMG Bitmapped GEM file format.

Integrated software Software that does more than one thing, usually word processing, database management, spreadsheet, telecommunications, and graphics.

Interactive Computer programs that require a human response. Noninteractive software (demo programs, for instance) will run without human intervention.

Interpreter A high-level programming language translator. It will take a single program statement separately and run it before going on to the next.

Joystick The handheld stick used for computer games and sometimes used as a menu control device.

JPEG For *J*oint *P*hotographic *E*xperts *G*roup; a standard for image compression.

Kerning A more refined method of letterspacing in which variable spacing between letters presents a more balanced or pleasing visual look when printing a document.

Landscape printing Printing text and graphics sideways (across the 11-inch width of an 8.5-inch by 11-inch paper). Opposite of portrait printing.

Layer Some graphics programs allow for an image to be manipulated by dividing its parts into separate layers. Each layer may be worked with independently, but the total image is a sum of all of the layers.

Layout setting A group of values that describes a printed page, such as tabs, margins, headers, columns, page numbers, etc.

Leading The amount of space between lines of print.

Letterspacing Space added between letters to prevent too much blank space between words in a line of justified print.

LMB Graphic file format used by DeluxePaint.

Local area network (LAN) A system that connects computers for the sharing of data, files, electronic mail, and expensive peripherals.

Memory A computer's ability to store and hold data. Data is usually stored temporarily in the computer's chips, or more permanently on hard or floppy disk drives.

Metafile A vector graphics format ideally suited for use on a computer screen during displays, presentations, etc.

Microcomputer A small desktop or home computer. The distinctions between the different sizes of computers blur more each year as the large ones decrease in size and the small ones increase in power.

Minicomputer   A medium-range computer in both capability and memory.

Modem   From the terms *mo*dulator/*dem*odulator, a device for translating the digital code of the computer into the analog code of the telephone line, and back again. Two modems (one at each end) are required for two computers to communicate over the telephone. Computers can be directly connected without modems if they are close enough to connect with a cable.

Monitor   The screen that displays the computer's answers or data.

Mouse   Small, handheld object that moves the cursor on the screen as the mouse is moved on a desktop.

Object-oriented graphics   Graphics that are represented and created by mathematical formulas. Opposite of bit-mapped graphics.

Off-the-shelf software   Software written for a very specific use, not modifiable to any great extent.

Online   Any peripheral device such as a printer that is in an active mode. Any computer network; i.e., any activity between two or more computers.

Optical character recognition (OCR)   The act of "reading" text from a printed page and translating it into ASCII text.

Paint program   Any graphics program that simulates various paint activities on the computer screen input through a graphics tablet, mouse, etc. The result is a raster (bitmapped) image.

Pantone   A color-matching process used for professional color printing.

Parallel transmission   One byte of data being sent as eight bits simultaneously.

Parameter   A setting for baud rate, parity, line feeds, etc., that determines how a device or computer will act. These parameters may be changed by the operator under software control or, sometimes, under hardware control with DIP switches, but they always have factory settings (defaults).

Parity   A method for checking the accuracy of data transmission by adding up the data bits to a total that must be either odd or even. If the proper addition is not made by the computer, the data is rejected and must be retransmitted.

Pattern fill   A paint tool that will fill a selected area with patterns taken from a palette.

PCX   A popular graphics file format from the ZSoft Corporation for handling bitmapped images.

Peripheral   Any device that is not part of the computer proper, whether internal or external to the computer housing. Peripheral devices include modems, printers, disk drives, and graphics tablets.

PICT   A graphic file format used in Macintosh Quickdraw toolbox for object-oriented graphics.

PICTOR   A graphic image compression system used to reduce transmission time of graphic files.

Pixel   One dot of a bitmapped graphic.

Point   A measurement for type in which 1 point equals 1/72 inch.

Portrait printing   Printing text and graphics in the usual manner, across the 8.5-inch width of an 8.5-inch by 11-inch paper. Opposite of landscape printing.

PostScript A page description language for microcomputers that has become a standard created by Adobe Systems, Inc. It is completely device-independent and can be used on many types of printers. Many laser printers come with PostScript built in. A PostScript document can be manipulated, enlarged, and changed in many ways.

Presentation graphic A graphic that displays business, sales, or numerical information; the best example of presentation graphics is the business graph or chart for use in business presentations.

Primary process colors The elemental colors of red, yellow, and blue that, when mixed together, form other colors.

Printer A device for printing out hardcopy of the computer results. Printers may be dot matrix, daisywheel, inkjet, and laser.

Protocol An agreed-upon method for data transmission that reduces the chance of error. For instance, if two computers are programmed to accept only incoming sets of data bits or signals that add up to an even number, one coming in as an odd number is judged incorrect and must be retransmitted (*see* Parity).

Public domain Software without copyright restrictions.

Pull-down menu A selection of choices that is always available by clicking the menu bar at the top of Windows or the Macintosh system. It retracts once the selection has been made.

Pull-quote Sometimes called a "callout." A statement taken from an article and emphasized in larger type to highlight some important point.

Random-access memory (RAM) Memory in a computer that changes as the computer uses it.

Raster image A bitmapped image.

Read-only memory (ROM) Memory that already has a program stored on it. The computer can read this memory or stored information but cannot change or add to it.

RIFF For *R*aster *I*mage *F*ile *F*ormat; used to store gray-scale images.

Runtime version Any program sold with and required by another program. For example, some programs require Windows to operate; if the user does not own Windows, a special runtime version may be available to achieve the same purpose. The runtime version will work only with that application.

Sans serif A style of typeface that has no short horizontal lines at the tops and bottoms of letters (serifs).

Scalable font A font that can be created in any required point size from one base font with the use of mathematical formulas. Bitmapped fonts, on the other hand, may look better, but require sets of each specific size on disk.

Scaling A technique used in presentation graphics to highlight differences in data.

Scanner A device that can digitize a photo or other image on paper for use with computers.

Screen capture A procedure that transfers the image on a computer screen to a text or graphics file.

Screen saver A utility program for preventing burn-in damage to computer monitors. The program maintains continuous action on screen to prevent static image damage. Many screen savers are very entertaining and worth having just for fun.

SDF For *S*tandard *D*ata *F*ormat; a file format that uses fixed-length fields to transfer data from one program to another.

Serif A small mark added to the tops and bottoms of letters to create typefaces.

Shareware Copyrighted software that is freely distributed. If the user wishes to continue to use it, a license fee must be remitted to the owner of the software, as stipulated in the software itself.

Shear A way to distort vertically or horizontally selected areas for computer imaging.

Softcopy Information sent to the computer screen, distinct from "hardcopy," which is printed out.

Software The invisible part of the computer; the set of instructions that tells the hardware what to do with the data it receives.

Spooler A method of sending data to a buffer or storage area to free up the computer or other device. For instance, by sending a long file to a buffer, the computer may continue to function without waiting; by sending a second file to the print buffer, a line or queue is formed waiting for the printer to finish.

Spray can A tool in desktop publishing that emulates a can of paint being sprayed on paper. The color and size can be controlled to produce differing effects on the computer "canvas."

Spreadsheet The electronic version of the accountant's pad. Formulas and data may be entered and the results calculated immediately. A second set of data or a change in any data element will result in a recalculation of the entire spreadsheet, making it possible to judge the effect of changes in budgets, for example, very quickly.

Stacking A form of layering in Designer in which newer objects in a design overlay older ones.

Style sheet A file that is a shorthand way of keeping track of layout settings such as columns, fonts, margins, etc. It can be very efficiently used from document to document.

Telecommunication Communication over long distances through telephone lines, satellite, or other means.

Telecommute The act of going to work at the terminal without having to physically go to the workplace.

Template A form, electronic or paper, that represents work someone has prepared but that may be used over and over with different sets of data. An example is the spreadsheet in which formulas have been placed for creating a budget. Since any two businesses that use the same kind of budget can use the same formulas, they can use the same template.

Terminal A place where people may interface with a computer through a keyboard, monitor, or printer. The computer need not be present; it can be reached through either the telephone lines with a modem or directly through cable (known as hardwiring) in a local area network.

Thumbnail A miniature representation of a page for purposes of seeing how it will look when it is actually printed.

TIFF   For *T*agged *I*mage *F*ile *F*ormat; an information-transfer format for graphic images that supports halftones, black-and-white data, dithered data, and grayscale.

Tool   In graphics programs, any special feature for manipulating text or graphics, such as line drawing, floods, fills, paintbrush, etc. Also frequently used as another name for utility programs.

Tracking   A form of kerning. Spaces between letters can be expanded or shortened by percentage factors.

Translator   A computer program that translates code from one computer program to another. It is especially useful for translating between programming languages.

TrueType   A Windows 3.1 and Macintosh System 7 scalable font system.

Type family   A group of related typefaces including bold, italic, etc.

Typeface   The design of type as opposed to its size or style such as bold, italic, etc.

Upload   To accept data into a computer. The opposite of "download," which is to send data to another computer.

User Group   Any group of people who get together for the purpose of exchanging information about computers, especially for problem solving. Such groups can host special events, such as having speakers or giving hardware/software demonstrations, or get group discounts on computers and supplies.

Utility   Often a program used for housekeeping, such as a typeface management system, data backup program, etc.

Virus   A destructive program that replicates itself to cause mischief.

Windows   A Graphical User Interface (GUI) that makes it possible to run several programs simultaneously. Each program has its own "window," hence the name. Windows is also characterized by its use of picture icons instead of file names to quickly move back and forth between applications on a graphical representation of a desktop.

Word processing   A software program that allows users to rearrange and revise text (sentences, words, etc.) without having to retype everything before hardcopy is produced. Often these programs come with "spellers" that check documents for suspect words (possibly misspelled words).

Workstation   An area that contains the necessary equipment (furniture, outlets, table, etc.) for work with a computer. Such places should have good lighting and comfortable seating.

WYSIWYG   For *what you see is what you get*; refers to the fact that some programs, in particular word processing and page layout programs, allow the user to see the exact representation of the page on the screen before it is printed out.

Zoom   A special effect with which objects on a screen can be enlarged or shrunk.

Index of Software

Patrick R. Dewey lives in Chicago, Illinois, with his two dogs, Software and Printer. He has written more than seventeen books on microcomputers, interactive fiction, fan clubs, and comic books. He is also the director of the Maywood Public Library District, and teaches a graduate course at Rosary College School of Library and Information Science. In his spare time he operates a model train layout in his basement and, in good weather, rides a skateboard around the Chicago Loop with young friends Timmy and Kevin.